Marie Géraldine Rademacher
Narcissistic Mothers in Modernist Literature

Lettre

to my husband

Marie Géraldine Rademacher works as post-doctoral researcher at the University of Tokyo in Japan. Her research focuses on Travel Writing written by European women who came to Japan in the early decade of the Twentieth century. She also teaches English Literature at Seikei University in Tokyo.

MARIE GÉRALDINE RADEMACHER
Narcissistic Mothers in Modernist Literature
New Perspectives on Motherhood in the Works of D.H. Lawrence,
James Joyce, Virginia Woolf, and Jean Rhys

[transcript]

D 188

Bibliographic information published by the Deutsche Nationalbibliothek
The Deutsche Nationalbibliothek lists this publication in the Deutsche Nationalbibliografie; detailed bibliographic data are available in the Internet at http://dnb.d-nb.de

© 2019 transcript Verlag, Bielefeld

All rights reserved. No part of this book may be reprinted or reproduced or utilized in any form or by any electronic, mechanical, or other means, now known or hereafter invented, including photocopying and recording, or in any information storage or retrieval system, without permission in writing from the publisher.

Cover layout: Kordula Röckenhaus, Bielefeld
Proofread by Prof. Steve Clark
Printed by Majuskel Medienproduktion GmbH, Wetzlar
Print-ISBN 978-3-8376-4966-6
PDF-ISBN 978-3-8394-4966-0
https://doi.org/10.14361/9783839449660

Contents

Acknowledgments | 7

1 An Overview of Motherhood | 9
Introduction | 9

2 Disentangling Notions | 15
2.1 Autobiographical Aspects | 15
2.2 The Origins of Narcissism | 26
2.3 Freudian Theory | 29
2.4 Sociological and Feminist Perspectives | 34
2.5 Narcissistic Mothers in Modernist Novels | 39

3 A Mother's Vision and Love in D.H. Lawrence's *Sons and Lovers* | 43
3.1 Mrs. Morel's Narcissistic Injury | 46
3.2 Mrs. Morel's Wounded Narcissism | 49
3.3 A Woman of Vision | 59
3.4 Exonerating the Mother | 65

4 Mothers and Social Criticism in James Joyce's *Dubliners* | 77
4.1 Mothers in "The Boarding House" and "A Mother" | 79
4.2 Mrs. Sinico's Emotional Empathy | 91

5   A Mother's 'Divided Self' in Virginia Woolf's
    To the Lighthouse | 105
5.1 A 'Blundered' Portrayal of Mrs. Ramsay | 107
5.2 Behind Self-Love Lurks the Love for Others | 115
5.3 Narcissism as Means for Self-Preservation | 125

6   "I'm a Cérébrale": A Mother's Isolation and
    Marginalization in Jean Rhys'
    Good Morning, Midnight | 133
6.1 Sasha's Narcissistic Injury | 134
6.2 On the Lookout for Reparative Measures | 140
6.3 The New Face of the 'Flâneur' | 146

7   From Modernism to Contemporary Literature:
    A Timeless Debate | 163
    Conclusion | 163

    Works Cited | 169

Acknowledgments

I would like to express my gratitude to my advisor Professor Cordula Lemke from Freie Universität Berlin for her continuous support of my Ph.D. studies and related research. Her valuable guidance helped me in all the time of research and writing of my dissertation, which developed into this book.

I am also grateful to Professor Steve Clark, who was my advisor during the time I spent at the University of Tokyo. I benefitted from his immense knowledge and his patience. His insightful comments and questions have allowed me to widen my research from various perspectives and have tremendously contributed to the creation of this work.

My sincere thanks also go to Professor Stefan Keppler-Tasaki, who gave me the opportunity to join the outstanding research facilities of the University of Tokyo and made this collaboration between the two universities feasible. Without his precious support it would not have been possible to complete this project.

Last but not least, I would like to thank my family: my husband, my parents and my sisters for their moral support and for encouraging me to persevere in this career path I chose years ago. I am grateful to my husband for wisely advising me and relentlessly helping me in this venture.

1 An Overview of Motherhood

INTRODUCTION

> Women mother. In our society, as in most societies, women not only bear children. They also take primary responsibility for infant care, spend more time with infants and children than do men, and sustain primary emotional ties with infants.
> *(Chodorow 1978: 3)*

Over the years, research conducted on motherhood has unanimously underlined the determining role that mothers play in the child's psychological and physical development. While psychoanalytic theories have been primarily concerned with the mother's unconscious and her strong attachment to the child, feminist perspectives have pointed out the oppression that women undergo, first biologically during pregnancy, and then socially when they are confined to their mothering role. Women's ability to bear children and the role they play in the child's growth and wellbeing have supported the largely accepted discourse on motherhood, which often tends to reduce them to the social role of selfless, protective nurturers who find maternal satisfaction through childcare. Glorifying representations of mother figures, especially in art and religion, have widely spread and sustained these images of motherhood. Mothers have been and continue to be praised for their important contribution in maintaining cultural values, as well as promoting state ideologies. However, if they fail to conform to these social expectations, they are often condemned and viewed as 'bad mothers' or in some cases even as 'deviant monsters'. Aware of these on-going debates surrounding the question of motherhood and the representation of mothers, this book examines under a new light the multi-faceted depiction of narcissistic mothers in Modernist literature, hence challenging the too often simplistic, dualistic mainstream conception of mothers as either devoted caretakers or selfishly neglectful parents. Even if 'narcissism' and 'motherhood' have often appeared incompatible and at times, also vigorously been attacked in previous work, as it implies women's withdrawal from their role as mothers, as well as from society, their association is still possible and the outcome, though undeniably contentious, can be in some cases more productive than problematic. The issue of narcissism is certainly not new in literature. However, its association with mother figures offers an unusual lens to observe and analyse the representation of motherhood in Modernist novels, which as a matter of fact abound with examples of narcissistic mother figures. Indeed, the Modernist period itself can be qualified as essentially narcissistic, since it strongly focuses on the individual's place in society, thereby striving to find "fresh ways of looking at man's position and function in the universe" (Gillies/Mahood 2007: 2). In fact, the 20th century has witnessed an important evolution of the European novel. Michael Bell comments that this change can be explained by the fact that "over this period, the importance of the individual, in increasing contrast to that of the social order, continued to rise to the point where society might be valued in so far as it serves the fulfilment of the individual rather than the other way around" (M. Bell 2001: 184). Therefore, in reflecting upon the place that the individual has come to occupy in society, following major socio-political changes and the outbreak of the First World War, psychoanalysts, philosophers and sociologists, such as Sigmund Freud and Karl Marx have shown concern for the question of the rationality of the human mind, while the German philosopher Friedrich Nietzsche has stressed human's "Machtgelüst" (Nietzsche 2017: 56) or 'desire for power'. It is through an examination of the following major Modernist novels – David Herbert Lawrence's *Sons and Lovers* (1913), James Joyce's *Dubliners* (1914), Virginia Woolf's *To the Lighthouse* (1927), and finally *Good Morning, Midnight* (1939) by Jean Rhys – that these notions of increasing self-awareness, darker aspects of human nature and excessive self-love are best illustrated. These novels feature mother figures who display many elements of narcissism as defined in the 'Diagnostic Criteria for Narcissistic Personality Disorder' (DSM-III), published by the American Psychiatric Association (APA) and are much more commonly used than the Freudian categories. It provides the standard features of specific mental disorders, in our case of 'Narcissistic Personality Disorder' (1980), which includes: "a grandiose sense of self-importance; preoccupation with fantasies of unlimited success, power, brilliance, beauty, or ideal love; exhibitionism; cool indifference or rage, inferiority, shame, and emptiness; entitlement, exploitativeness, overidealization, or devaluation; and lack of empathy" (Morrison 1986: 2). Yet, these novels reveal that these women occasionally also show motherly concern for their offspring. They demonstrate that the picture is more complex than the crudely judgemental definition of 'Narcissistic Personality Disorder' would suggest and they show that narcissism and motherhood can and actually 'do' frequently co-exist without necessarily resulting in damaging effects on the child. Perhaps here, we can speak of benevolent narcissistic mothers, a concept which fundamentally challenges the ideal image of romantic motherhood and the myth of selfless mothers. From its very beginnings, psychoanalysis has used literature as a kind of empirical verification (e.g. Ernest Jones' famous essay "Hamlet and Oedipus" or *Sons and Lovers*) and is now probably more influential in literary studies than clinical diagnosis. Jeffrey Berman points out the existence of an interconnection between the artist and the psychoanalyst, a link that has been established by Sigmund Freud himself in his *Introductory Lectures on Psychoanalysis* (1916), in which he claims that the artist is "in rudiments an introvert, not far removed from neurosis" and that he "desires to win honour, power, wealth, fame and the love of women; but he lacks the means for achieving these satisfactions" (Freud 1916: 375). Consequently, the artist will seek a substitute gratification through art, and according to Freud's observation, there exists a major link between creativity and suffering. In the case of D.H. Lawrence, James Joyce, Virginia Woolf and Jean Rhys, biographers have documented feelings of anxiety occasioned by the mother's absence/death, leading to a state of mourning for the lost love-object as well as depression, and these issues clearly pervade their work. Therefore, it is important to acknowledge the autobiographical elements permeating the four texts under scrutiny without, however, claiming to conduct a faithful psychoanalytical analysis of the authors' actual mothers, although it is difficult not to refer to this context occasionally, for the richness of the text stems from the artist's ability to draw inspiration from his/her environment and enhance it with creativity. Freud's influence on Lawrence, Joyce, Woolf and Rhys is undeniable; by seeking to dismiss the traditional realist novel, which they felt was inadequate to capture the complexity of human existence, these Modernist writers choose to adopt new narrative techniques to represent the working of human subjectivity. Whether they explicitly admit it or not, they have to some extent, integrated either consciously or unconsciously the Freudian psychoanalytic perspective in their depiction of the meanders of a 'troubled' mind. Freud's writings had a subsequent influence on literature as the poet W. H. Auden indicates when he wrote of Freud that: "If often he was wrong, and, at times, absurd / to us he is no more a person / now but a whole climate of opinion / under which we conduct our different lives" (Auden 1976: 275). Jean Rhys' *Good Morning, Midnight* represents, as Lilian Pizzichini observes, "a daring break with conventional narrative", a novel which demands from its reader to "read the novel the way Sasha experiences life: fractured, bewildering, with a hint of menace" (Pizzichini 2009: 217). Rhys' use of elliptical prose parallels James Joyce's invitation to go beyond the words and silences in order to decipher his short stories, while D.H. Lawrence's use of multiple narrative voices reflects

Freud's conception of 'mind' that he regards as constituted of two distinct divided spaces, namely consciousness and subconsciousness. Rick Rylance supports this idea through his statement that *Sons and Lovers* is "concerned, very urgently with the relations of mind and body" (Rylance 2001: 27). This perception of the psyche is also illustrated in Woolf's writing through the recurrent image of the mind as a container of thoughts, feelings and sensation, for instance in *To the Lighthouse* through the metaphorical allusion to "a pool of thought, a deep basin of reality" (Woolf 2006: 147). These innovative narrative techniques were certainly connected with the unprecedented social and political developments, culminating in the major upheaval occasioned by the Great War and later on the Second World War, which drove these writers to reflect upon the questions of human existence and conditions, thereby intersecting with Freud's ideas of an individual's sense of self. Even if the influence of Freud's psychoanalytic theories on these writers has been recognized, this book, while informed by a Freudian theoretical reading, does not attempt to carry out an intellectual source study. Finally, besides the influence of psychoanalytic theories on Modernist literature, it is also essential to acknowledge the contribution of gender studies to the question of motherhood. Nancy Chodorow's and Julia Kristeva's work turns out to be inevitably influenced by psychoanalysis, hence emphasizing the existence of an interdependence between narcissism and the Oedipal narrative. Narcissistic mothers seem to sustain their sons' Oedipal complex, through their excessive emotional attachment to their children, who in turn receive gratification from being adored and admired by the loved one. The selected Modernist novels contribute to exemplifying different forms of narcissism, by contrasting the image of self-absorbed mothers who eventually redirect their love onto their children, to the masculine attitude (mainly embodied through James Duffy in Joyce's "A Painful Case" and Paul Morel in Lawrence's *Sons and Lovers*), which remains focused on the ego. In Virginia Woolf's and Jean Rhys' narrative, the masculine form of narcissism becomes the expression of excessive self-interest and selfishness leading to a sense of grandiosity and superiority, which parallels the launch of the two World Wars the 20th century has witnessed. Additionally, these novels demonstrate that while narcissism as a diagnosis of individuals may be problematic, it however works well as a model of collective consciousness.

2 Disentangling Notions

2.1 AUTOBIOGRAPHICAL ASPECTS

Moving away from Gustave Flaubert's model of 'impersonality', which insists on "the disappearance of the author from his work" (Conlon 1982:129) and advocates the unobtrusive subjectivity of the narrator in the story, these Modernist writers aspire to a much more fluid concept of life-writing by drawing from their personal experience. Indeed, Richard Ellmann, James Joyce's biographer, once wrote that:

> The life of an artist ... differs from the lives of other persons in that its events are becoming artistic sources even as they command his present attention. Instead of allowing each day, pushed back by the next, to lapse into imprecise memory, he shapes again the experiences which have shaped him. He is at once the captive and the liberator. (Ellmann 1982: 3)

His observation suggests the existence of a strong interconnection between the writer's life and his work and therefore calls for a brief reference to the autobiographical components present in the four Modernist novels examined in this book. When it comes to D.H. Lawrence, Harry Moore confirms that Lawrence himself underlines the closeness of life and art in *Sons and Lovers*, acknowledging that "towards the end of his life that the first half of the book was all autobiography" (Moore 1951: 94). On November 1910, as his mother was about to die,

D.H. Lawrence confessed in a letter to the Scottish poet, Rachel A. Taylor of his intense attachment to his mother, comparable to one between "great lovers" (Boulton 2002: 187) and recognizes that this strong affection has interfered with his relationships with other women, as well as with his father, Arthur Lawrence. The writer's ambivalent feelings towards his father are clearly expressed through his realization of the latter's "warmth" and "tenderness" (Worthen 1992: 59), while he expresses hatred for the man, he believed mistreated his mother. This led Joyce critics to focus on father-son (Ulysses-Telemachus) relationship, despite the fact that Stephen Dedalus is haunted by his mother's ghost. Yet, his statement that "I was born hating my father" (Tedlock 1965: 14) implicitly indicates Lawrence's awareness of Lydia's influence on her son's perception. This underlying internal conflict is reflected through his works, principally in *Sons and Lovers*. William Edward Hopkin agrees that "the greatest single influence in Lawrence's life was his devotion to his mother" (Hopkin 1957: 23), who turns out to be a source of inspiration in his work. By writing *Sons and Lovers* and other mother poems, for instance "The Virgin Mother" (Lawrence 1994: 67) or "Monologue of a Mother" (Lawrence 1994: 14-15), Judith Farr notes that "the young Lawrence acknowledged his mother as muse, fostering his writing and painting" (Farr 1990: 195). Clearly, his novel has been inspired by his relationship with his mother. The autobiographical elements in the narrative are easy to identify: first, his relationship with his father was very much like Paul Morel's, with phases of extreme aversion and hostility towards Walter Morel/Arthur Lawrence. Then, his deep love for his mother echoes Paul's intense affection for Gertrude Morel. Lawrence himself sided with his mother; she was passionately fond of him; they clung to each other like lovers would. He cared about what his mother thought of him, both as a man and an artist, and tried his best to please her. Also, in October 1901, he lost his brother, William Ernest. Then, both Lawrence and his sister, Ada, took care of their mother on her death bed. The author experienced this as a traumatic event. He recalls:

Then in that year, for me everything collapsed, save the mystery of death, and the haunting of death in life. I was twenty-five, and from the death of my mother [9 December 1910], the world began to dissolve around me, beautiful, iridescent, but passing away substanceless. Till I almost dissolved away myself, and was very ill: when I was twenty-six. (Lawrence 1994: 623)

Later, Lawrence himself came to realize that *Sons and Lovers*, which mainly focuses on the bond between mother and sons, against the father and later the sons' sweethearts, is based on a distorted truth, aiming at "mak[ing] Paul and his mother come out of it better than they should, at the expense of Miriam and his father" (Sagar 1989: 11), which Lawrence had not realized at the time he was writing the book. But with hindsight, Lawrence admitted he has been harsh on his father, who he saw mainly through his mother's eyes and this accounts for the presence of multiple narrative voices in *Sons and Lovers*. Lawrence's either conscious or unconscious ambivalent feelings towards his parents are revealed in his novel, through his use of a variety of narrative voices, which reflect his mixed intentions, for at times he nuances the portrayal of the drunk father with one of "a gentle soul, who marvelled at his child's development in the world" (Spencer 1980: 40). Then, Paul Morel, who in spite of his excessive love for his mother, on many occasions, recognizes that she "bore him, loved him, kept him ... so that he could not be free to go forward with his own life, really love another woman" (Lawrence 1992: 389).

If D.H. Lawrence's works were influenced by his conflictual relationships with his mother, James Joyce also undoubtedly drew inspiration from distressing familial situations which obviously marked him throughout his life. The family in his work is often represented as a fragile unit, revolving around the mother and which could potentially collapse at any time. The Joyce family itself was constantly threatened with breaking apart, a condition worsened by the financial hardship they had to face. And for their social decline from comfortable middle-class status to genuine poverty, John Joyce was to be blamed. His children hated him for his failure to fulfil his role of head of the household and provider for the family. This image of the father as withdrawn from his family duty and the picture of the tenacious mother appear recurrently in Joyce's writing, for instance in *Dubliners*, and principally in the three short stories examined in chapter four. Also, along with family discord and the burden of financial insecurity, James Joyce experiences physical displacement caused by frequently moving from house to house. This prevented him from developing any attachment to a place in particular. It is in the year 1891 that the Joyce family experienced the harshness of the financial crisis, which resulted in them having to move out of their home in Bray (an upscale seaside resort in County Wicklow about ten miles south of the city) to a house in Carysfort Avenue on the south side, before a further removal to the north side of the river Liffey. The river, Terence Brown notes, "marked [...] a social divide between the indisputably respectable and the doubtfully so" (Brown 1992: xi). Therefore, Joyce who until then had enjoyed the pleasant neighbourhood of Bray became exposed to the poor dwellings, houses of ill-repute, lower-middle-class desperation and severe poverty of Dublin, hence discovering a new aspect of life in the city. However, Hélène Cixous explains, Joyce "became accustomed to insecurity, and probably profited from it in the form of experience to be used artistically; the difficulty of everyday life led him to the building of imaginary replacements" (Cixous 1972: 4). Besides the troubles occasioned by poverty, James Joyce was also confronted to the "underhand pressures exerted by the Church via the mother" (Cixous 1972: 7). In fact, Joyce uses the economic and social problems he encounters for the purpose of art. It is through his novels and mainly in his autobiographical book *Stephen Hero* that the reader is granted access to the personality hidden behind the writer's pen. *Stephen Hero*, Gorman observes, serves as:

> a personal history ... of the growth of mind, his [James Joyce's] own mind, and his own intensive absorption in himself and what he had been and how he had grown out of the Jesuitical garden of

his youth. He endeavoured to see himself objectively, to assume a godlike poison of watchfulness over the small boy and youth he called Stephen and who was really himself. (Gorman 1941: 133)

In *Portrait of the Artist as a Young Man*, Joyce portrays Stephen Dedalus, a fictional alter ego of Joyce himself, as a rebellious son who despises his selfish father and disagrees with his mother's blind religious faith. Both father and son were made responsible for May's (Joyce's mother) early death, the former for his cruelty, and the latter for his rejection of the Catholic faith. However, besides the prevailing tension between mother and son, Joyce did love and need her, erratically showing paralyzing emotional attachment to her. Cixous confirms that:

> His [James Joyce] mother-fixation is clear: on the one hand he cannot do without her, he needs her to participate in his most private life, to obtain her approval; and on the other, he is always tenderly careful and solicitous, without going as far as self-sacrifice, in her interests. Filial and paternal in his attitude towards her, he cannot but associate her image in his mind with those of mourning, death, and Ireland in the guise of the "poor old woman" carrying milk who appears in "Telemachus". The mother-fixation reveals an ambiguity of feelings, of simultaneous guilt and mistrust. (Cixous 1972: 22)

However, even if great tension existed between Joyce and his mother to the extent that he chooses to depict her as a hated haunting ghost in his novels, May's letters to Joyce and the testimony of other family members demonstrate that she was devoted to him until her death and that he did passionately love her, profoundly suffering when she passed away. Mourning for his dead mother led Joyce to look for substitutes through his Aunt Josephine (towards whom he turned all his affection), Harriet Weaver (Joyce's patron) and finally Nora Barnacle, who he eventually married in 1931. Joyce's personal search for an adoptive mother certainly inspired the shaping of his protagonists, for instance Mr. Duffy in "A Painful Case", whose love affair with an elderly woman has the characteristics of a relationship between mother and son. Indeed, Joyce used his personal affliction and experiences for the purpose of art, and as Cixous points out, he used them in such a way that "a private grievance of his may become relevant for everyman" (Cixous 1972: xv).

As for Virginia Woolf's novel *To the Lighthouse*, critics have largely agreed on the autobiographical aspect of the text, which they believe was written in the hope it "would modulate her obsessive preoccupation with her parents" (Panken 1987: 1), especially with her mother, Julia Stephen by whom the character of Mrs. Ramsay was essentially inspired. The depiction of the affectionate Mrs. Ramsay, based on Virginia Woolf's own memory of Julia Stephen, reflects her admiration for her mother, who she loved with the intensity of an "unrequited lover" (ibd.), but simultaneously who she remembered as being elusive while she lived. Then, when on May, 5th 1895 Julia Stephen died after contracting rheumatic fever, she left behind a thirteen-year-old daughter who experienced her mother's death as "the greatest disaster that could happen" (Woolf 1976: 40). Viviane Forrester explains that "dead or living, she [Julia] slipped away, became the very essence of lack" and that in 1939, at the dawn of World War II, "Virginia was still searching for that perpetually lost mother" (Forrester 2015: 70). Besides Julia's maternal withdrawal when she was still alive, her tragic death was certainly devastating for the whole family and proved to be the source of Woolf's long-lasting grief. For many years after her mother's death and until she wrote *To the Lighthouse*, at forty-four, "Virginia Woolf could not live – could not write, or act, or think – without measuring herself by her mother" (I. Bell 1986: 150). She confessed that "the presence of my mother obsessed me. I could hear her voice, see her imagine what she would do or say as I went my day's doings" (ibd.). However, despite her boundless affection for Julia and her acknowledgment of her dedication to her children, Woolf could not help seeing her mother critically. Describing her as "quick-tempered", "impetuous" or again "imperious" (Woolf 1976: 38-39), she stressed her mother's austerity and condemned her disproportionate admiration for her husband's achievement at the expense of her children, who felt neglected and ended up directing their anger toward their needy father. Woolf admitted: "we made him the type of all that we hated in our lives; he was the tyrant of inconceivable selfishness, who had replaced the beauty and merriment of the dead with ugliness and gloom" (Woolf 1976: 56). Ilona Bell confirms that "as a bereft and oppressed daughter, Woolf idealized her mother and abhorred her father" (I. Bell 1986: 153), but she knew that her image of both parents was often exaggerated. Therefore, if in *To the Lighthouse*, Woolf draws a portrait of a tyrannical father through the character of Mr. Ramsay, evidence from her letters, diaries and various written works shows that she still contradictorily retained a fascination with Leslie Stephen, who played an important part in shaping his daughter's imagination through the education he gave her and through his own works. Lyndall Gordon points out, "near the end of her life she could still see her father from two angles at once: 'As a child condemning; as a woman of 58 understanding – I should say tolerating'" (Gordon 1984: 17). Woolf's conflicting feelings for her father are best reflected through the portrait of Mr. Ramsay, who she depicts as tyrannical and demanding, but at the same time sentimental, as William Bankes' memory of his old friend treasuring the sight of little chicks and exclaiming "Pretty-pretty" (Woolf 2009: 20) suggests. Also, the first part of *To the Lighthouse*, which ends on the harmonious image of the parents as they read together, emphasizes the intensity of their love for each other. Consequently, when his wife died, Leslie's mental health rapidly deteriorated, for it was directly linked to his wife's. He completely depended on her, constantly seeking comfort and encouragement from Julia and thinking of himself as a "skinless man" (Q. Bell 1973: 38) when deprived of her presence and her ministrations. He believed that "nothing was to touch him save her soothing and healing hand" (Woolf 1976: 80). Therefore, Quentin Bell remarks "essentially the happiness of the Stephen home derived from the fact that the children knew their parents to be so deeply and happily in love" (Q. Bell 1973: 38). As a result, Julia's death happened to change the family relationship as Woolf came to recognize in her novel, when she admits that the Stephen's household was to be turned into "a house full of unrelated passions" (Woolf 2006: 123). If Leslie suffered from his wife's absence, he was not the only one. Virginia Woolf, as many critics observed, "never fully released her 'reservoir' of pain" (Panken 1987: 11). She was unable to mourn her mother's death and "her grieving process was [therefore] never completed" (ibd.) and it seems that in the loss of her mother the issues of identity and fusion are raised. For instance, Susan M. and Edward J. Kenney (1982) underlined Woolf's inability to "move forward out of childhood", while Strouse emphasized Woolf's longing for "oneness with her mother" (Panken 1987: 11). Consequently, Woolf's attempt to create an integrated identity and to finally solve her separation-individuation issues is best reflected in "the psychological or metaphorical substrate of her autobiographical writing, in letters, diary, and memoirs, as well as in her fiction" (Panken 1987: 13). However, not only does *To the Lighthouse* provide essential autobiographical insights, but it also endorses a cathartic function for the author, who admitted undergoing a feeling of liberation and transformation once she finished putting pen to paper. Woolf explains that "I wrote the book very quickly; and when it was written, I ceased to be obsessed by my mother. I no longer hear her voice; I do not see her" (Woolf 1976: 81). She admits that "I did for myself what psycho-analysts do for their patients. I expressed some very long felt and deeply felt emotion" (ibd.). Here, Woolf confesses that her novel has allowed her to mourn her mother, a process mainly mirrored through the narration of Mrs. Ramsay's death. Woolf, who felt abandoned by her mother, illustrates first her frustration and indignation through the laconic and casual reference to Mrs. Ramsay's abrupt death, announced in brackets, and which seems almost vengeful. At the same time her stylistic narratorial choice anticipates the possible resolution of the daughter's conflict, for if at first we are tempted to understand her novel as being all about Mrs. Ramsay around whom the other characters seem to revolve, by the end, it becomes clear that the novel is also about the resolution of Lily Briscoe's (Mrs. Ramsay's substitute daughter) mother issues as the completion of her painting seems to suggest. This idea is confirmed by Hermione Lee's claim that *To the Lighthouse* "is above all about how the daughter can bring the mother back and let her go, can go beyond the pain and rage of her loss [...] to the possibility of loving but not needing her" (Lee 1996: 80). Moreover, although Woolf's memory of Talland House, in Cornwall where the Stephens have spent numerous holidays, has certainly inspired the description of the Ramsay's summer home in the Hebrides, Woolf has chosen to set her novel in Scotland, a choice which possibly speaks for her desire to come to terms with some painful childhood memories.

Finally, Jean Rhys grew up with a feeling of being unwanted. She had the impression that she was only a poor substitute for her parents' loss of their first child. Lilian Pizzichini remarks, "she [Jean Rhys] would carry this feeling of insubstantiality with her into adulthood" and that "as she grew, her mother's inattentiveness and mournful demeanour had far-reaching effects" (Pizzichini 2009: 7). Still, Jean Rhys kept some pleasant, happy childhood memories, for instance enjoying the exclusive attention and affection of her parents. She remembered sitting "crowned, bursting with pride and importance, safe, protected, sitting in a large armchair, my father on one side, my mother on the other, my shiny shoes a long way off the ground" (Rhys 2016: 7). However, four months later Brenda, Jean's younger sister was born and soon she felt everything changed. She believed, Lilian Pizzichini observes, that "her mother did not like her any more" (Pizzichini 2009: 16). This feeling is expressed through her heroine Julia in *After Leaving Mr Mackenzie*, whose "mother had been the warm centre of the world ... But suddenly she was 'entirely wrapped up in the new baby'" (Rhys 1985: 294-295). Then, by the time she turns eight or nine, she became aware of some changes in her appearance, which left her with the feeling of being singled out from her siblings, for she was pale, thin and fair, while the others were all dark and sturdy. Since Minna, Rhys' mother, was mainly preoccupied with the new baby, she had a nurse named Meta hired to look after Jean, who remembers that Meta delighted in playing tricks on the child, threatening and frightening her. One vivid example occurred when aged seven or eight, Jean was called by the nurse to the kitchen, where she was awaiting the girl, wearing a carnival mask, talking in a high-pitched voice and suddenly sticking her tongue out of the mask. Rhys, recalling this grotesque situation, tells that "when I saw the long tongue protruding idiotically under the blank eyes, I went into a fit of hysterics and had to be put to bed and pacified by a handkerchief saturated with eau-de-cologne tied around my head" (Angier 1992: 12). It was certainly a traumatic episode of her childhood, which later on was featured in her novels. Up to this point, the mother figures in Rhys' life have failed in providing the ministrations and affection the child longed for. Not only did she feel neglected, but her jealousy for Brenda led Jean to adopt a defiant and rebellious attitude as a statement of her pride, which slowly also turned out to be the expression of Rhys' own self-punishment. This is best represented through the incident of the two dolls, a dark one and a fair one, which arrived from England. She recollects strongly desiring the former "as I have never wanted anything in my life before" (Rhys 2006: 23) but her little sister wanted the dark one too, and eventually her mother made Rhys give it to Brenda. Jean remembered: "I laid the fair doll down. Her eyes were shut. Then I searched for a big stone, brought it down with all my force on her face and heard the smashing sound with delight" (Rhys 2006: 23-24). Her action of savagely destroying the toy reveals her desire "to destroy her 'fair', her outcast self", just like her heroine Antoinette in *Wide Sargasso Sea* destroys herself and feels a similar exultation, for it constitutes "a revenge on the rejecting world, and an escape from loneliness and madness" (Angier 1992: 15). At the same time, her act was also "an act of rebellion against her mother" (Pizzichini 2009: 31-32), who used to play the role of censor, and constantly reprimanded her, disapproved of her and tried to turn her into someone she was not. Later, Mina Rees Williams will inspire the mother figures in Rhys' novels, for instance in *Wide Sargasso Sea*, where the mother only desires her son and pushes her daughter away, ordering her to leave her alone. Then in *Good Morning, Midnight*, Lise is terrified of her mother for "when she was a little girl her mother beat her. For anything, for nothing" (Rhys 2000: 112). If these childhood episodes and her relationship with her mother have influenced Rhys' novels, when she writes about motherhood she also draws from her own experience. When she was in England, she experienced living a life as a demimondaine. She became the mistress of a wealthy stockbroker Lancelot Grey Hugh Smith, who she madly loved and who remained an occasional source of financial help to Rhys even after he ended their relationship. She had many love affairs and experienced the joy of pregnancy and motherhood in all its aspects, for instance when she had to go through an almost fatal and disheartening abortion. Then later, she lost her son William Owen as he was only three weeks old. She also experienced the pain of being deprived of her daughter Maryvonne following her separation from her husband John Lenglet. The death of her newborn child constituted a traumatic episode in the writer's life, an incident which she recounts for instance in *Good Morning, Midnight* and was without doubt the grief of her life, which she felt partly responsible for. Therefore, confronted by the challenges of maternity/motherhood from different angles, Jean Rhys was able to draw from her previous experiences and thus, provided a vivid, powerful portrayal of mother figures in her novels. Lilian Pizzichini confirms that Jean Rhys "would write about men and women and mothers and daughters for the rest of her life; about loss, the fear of loss and the inability to recover from loss because there is nothing that will compensate for what is gone" (Pizzichini 2009: 44). Surely, much of *Good Morning, Midnight* is inspired by her life in Paris, her painful marriage, her son's death and the multiple encounters she made. Yet, if the presence of autobiographical elements in these four Modernist novels should be acknowledged, it is important to keep in mind that these narratives were equally inspired by the writers' brilliant imagination and personal interpretation, and that these texts can also be read in the light of Sigmund Freud's psychanalytic theories on narcissism as well as Ovid's myth of Narcissus, which is prior to and in many ways more complex than the clinical diagnosis.

2.2 THE ORIGINS OF NARCISSISM

> Lay like a marble statue staring down.
> He gazes at his eyes, twin constellations,
> [...]
> Himself he longs for, longs unwittingly,
> Praising is praised, desiring is desired,
> And love he kindles while with love he burns.
> How often in vain he kissed the cheating pool
> And in the water sank his arms to clasp
> The neck he saw, but could not clasp himself!
> Not knowing what he sees, he adores the sight;
> That false face fools and fuels his delight.
> (B. Bloom 1990: 51)

The myth of Narcissus has pervaded literature for centuries, through endless retellings and adaptations. Commonly known as the story of a beautiful, self-absorbed, young man who fell deeply in love with his reflection in the water, the legend of Narcissus became the symbol for a sterile, self-centred love that results in a tragic death. However, Ovid's character reveals himself to be more than just a popular literary figure; he also turns out to provide a fertile ground for psychoanalytical interpretations, mainly a pre-Oedipal reading of the myth, focusing essentially on the child's desire to recover a lost maternal love and his quest for identity. It is important to mention that Narcissus' birth was the result of the rape of the water-lady, Liriope by Cephisus, who in his action almost drowned her in the stream. When taking a close look at Narcissus' fate, a parallelism can be established between his attraction to water and his mother's near drowning. Critics such as Hyman Spotnitz and Philip Resnikoff interpret Narcissus' obsessive gazing at the water as an expression of his intense longing for the maternal body: "Narcissus by identification with Cephisus was predestined also to seek the love object in water. Hence, part of the fascination exerted on Narcissus by the image he saw reflected in the pool stemmed from his incestuous strivings, i.e. his yearning for his mother" (Berman 1990: 6). Therefore, Narcissus' quest for identity and self-esteem urges him to look for maternal mirroring and validation from external objects. However, at the same time as he seeks maternal love, as shown by his attitude towards Echo, the mountain nymph who fell in love with him, Narcissus' vehement rejection "Hand off! Embrace me not!" repeats his mother's traumatic sexual union with Cephisus who we are told "embraced" and "ravished" Liriope in a winding brook. Berman suggests that Narcissus "seems to be projecting onto Echo an image of an assaultive, smothering mother whose touch threatens to absorb or devour his identity" (Berman 1990: 7). Narcissus embodies a son's ambivalence towards the maternal figure that he fears but at the same time desires. Berman observes that both overloved and underloved, Narcissus in turn becomes overloving and underloving and that these "typical narcissistic problems, often arise from parents who are alternately overinvolved and underinvolved with their children" (ibd.). He further explains that "overloving parents tend to be possessive, anxiously protective, and infantilizing; hence they prevent their children from achieving autonomy and independence" (ibd.). Additionally, in the case of Narcissus, the presence of the pre-Oedipal father, who plays a decisive part in the infant's separation from the mother is negated, hence further accounting for the son's inability to individuate from the symbiotic mother. In fact, the tragic story of Narcissus has proven to possess psychological complexity, which inspired clinical research on the issue of narcissism. This resulted in the awareness that narcissism could in some cases be a personality disorder. As a result, Freudian concepts have tended to be regarded increasingly sceptically in the recent decades, but a leap back to the mythic tradition of 'Echo and Narcissus', which dramatizes the issue of self-love and self-absorption, also demonstrates strongly positive elements and hence resists any simple reduction of 'narcissism' to a pathological condition. A more optimistic reading of the myth suggests that Narcissus' attraction to his reflection in the water could indicate his wish to reunite his two complementary halves, thereby, it addresses the problem of identification and reunification. Read in the light of Plato's ideals of self-knowledge, the text embodies the idea that knowledge of the soul can only be reached through *eros* (or love). In his *Symposium*, Plato describes the process of gaining self-knowledge through the mirrored sight. He compares the eye to a mirror and concludes that "the lover, looking into the best part of the eyes of the beloved, sees the best part of himself reflected there" (Boulding 2013: 3). Consequently, the individual has access to self-knowledge through enhancing one's self-esteem, primarily "through seeing the most beautiful and divine part of one's soul mirrored in a lover's eyes" (Boulding 2013: 9). Plato's reading of Narcissus is centered on productive love and fertility, for "love wants to possess the good forever" (Plato 1989: 54), which goes hand in hand with "giving birth in beauty" (Plato 1989: 53). Kaitlyn Boulding points out that "reproduction is the closest that mortals get to immortality. The lover wants his children, birthed ideas, and self to become beautiful" (Boulding 2013: 9). Therefore, according to Plato's ideals, self-knowledge arouses from falling in love with the most beautiful and divine part of one's self as reflected in the eyes of the lover, which is revealed to positively impact on the individual's self-esteem, leading him or her to seek immortality as the reincarnation of Narcissus into a flower suggests. Interpretations of the myth are endless as well as contradictory. Ovid's myth of Echo and Narcissus does not represent self-love strictly as unfavourable, but it also seems to acknowledge the moment of self-recognition through self-valuation as positive and necessary in an individual's development. This aspect is further explored in psychoanalysis mainly through Sigmund Freud's work on narcissism.

2.3 FREUDIAN THEORY

In 1898, Havelock Ellis was the first to draw a connection between the figure of Narcissus and the term 'narcissism'. It is in his paper entitled "Auto-Erotism: A Psychological Study", that he uses the term of 'Narcissus-like tendency' to designate an extreme form of autoeroticism, defined as a tendency "to cover all the spontaneous manifestations of the sexual impulse in the absence of a definite outer object to evoke them" (Ellis 1942: 362). A year later, in 1899, the German psychiatrist Paul Näcke chose the term 'narcissism' to refer to a sexual attitude in which "a person treats his own body in the same way in which the body of a sexual object is ordinarily treated-who looks at it, that is to say, strokes it and fondles it till he obtains complete satisfaction through these activities" (Freud 2013: 3). For Näcke, the term 'narcissism' came to describe a sexual perversion. But it is in 1914 that the concept was significantly elaborated by Sigmund Freud in his essay "On Narcissism: An Introduction" which continues to this day to be considered as a landmark contribution to the work of psychoanalysis. Freud observes that the narcissistic attitude is found in many individuals who suffer from other disorders. Freud came to the conclusion that narcissism might be present more commonly and even play a major role in human sexual development. Accordingly, he argues that "narcissism in this sense would not be a perversion, but the libidinal complement of the egoism of the instinct of self-preservation, a measure of which may justifiably be attributed to every living creature" (Freud 2013: 2). Here, Freud suggests the existence of a primary and 'normal' narcissism (as he puts it himself), a concept which arises from his work with patients who suffer from schizophrenia and dementia praecox, and who display these two main features: megalomania and withdrawal of their own interest from people and things of the external world. In that case, Freud explains "the libido that has been withdrawn from the external world has been redirected to the ego and thus gives rise to an attitude which may be called narcissism" (Freud 2013: 5). From his conclusion, it is essential to note Freud's distinction between two types of libido, namely 'ego-libido' (self) and 'object-libido' (people and things in the external world). Freud claims that "the more of the one is employed, the more the other become depleted" and that "the highest phase of development of which object-libido is capable is seen in the state of being in love, when the subject seems to give up his own personality in favour of an object-cathexis" (Freud 2013: 6). However, in the case of a person who is afflicted by pain and discomfort, the individual will most likely withdraw his interest from the external world as long as it is not concerned with his suffering. To illustrate this idea, Freud refers to the German poet Wilhelm Busch who describes the state of a poet suffering from a toothache. He writes "concentrate is his soul / in his molar's narrow hole" (Freud 2013: 15). Freud observes that "libido and ego-interest share the same fate and are once more indistinguishable from each other. The familiar egoism of the sick person covers both" (ibd.). As long as he is in pain, the poet redirects his 'libidinal cathexes' on his own ego, and later on, once he has recovered, switches back to external objects. Then questioning what makes it necessary to go beyond the limits of narcissism and redirect our libido to objects, Freud on the one hand acknowledges strong egoism as a means for self-preservation, a protection against falling ill. However, on the other hand, he recognizes, at last, the importance to "begin to love in order not to fall ill" and he believes that the individual is likely to become ill if, "in consequence of frustration, he is unable to love" (Freud 2013: 20). Here, Freud's thoughts appear to be contradictory. While on the one hand he is convinced that withdrawing the libido from the external world and redirecting it on the ego can be seen as a regression from true object relationship, (which he defines as 'secondary narcissism'), on the other hand he also seems to recognize that it can be seen as a means for self-preservation. As a result, it is difficult to conceive 'secondary narcissism' in strictly negative terms. Yet, Freud points out that in a love-relationship not being loved lowers one's self-esteem, while being loved raises it, hence once again "the aim and the satisfaction in a narcissistic object-choice is to be loved" (Freud 2013: 37-38). He further explains that a person in love is humble, because a person who loves, has given up a part of his narcissism and it can only be replaced by being loved in return. He was convinced that in order for the ego to develop, the individual has to depart from primary narcissism, by displacing the libido on to an ego ideal. He states that:

> Loving in itself, in so far as it involves longing and deprivation, lowers self-regard; whereas being loved, having one's love returned, and possessing the loved object raises it once more. When libido is repressed, the erotic cathexis is felt as a severe depletion of the ego, the satisfaction of love is impossible, and the reenrichment of the ego can be effected only by a withdrawal of libido from its objects. The return of the object-libido to the ego and its transformation into narcissism represents, as it were, a happy love once more; and, on the other hand, it is also true that a real happy love corresponds to the primal condition in which object-libido and ego-libido cannot be distinguished. (Freud 2013: 39-40)

Yet, in his study on narcissism, Freud proposes that another way to approach this issue is by observing the erotic life of human beings, namely through the object-choice of infants and growing children. He assumes that narcissism exists as early as the infant has a vague awareness of himself. From the beginning, he recognizes the importance of the mother in a child's 'optimal development' when he states that a child has two sexual objects, himself and the woman who nurses him, therefore postulating a primary narcissism in everyone. His idea of 'optimal development' remains problematic as it easily slides into censorious judgement on failed individuation. He claims that the choice of the mother or substitute mother as a child's primary love object derives from the fact that "the first auto-erotic sexual satisfactions are experienced in connection with vital functions which serve the purpose of self-preservation" (Freud 2013: 22), therefore a child becomes firstly attached to the person who is responsible for his or her feeding, care, and protection. This type of object-choice relationship has been identified as the 'anaclitic' or 'attachment' type. Meanwhile, he came across a second type, that of individuals whose libidinal development has been subjected to some disturbance, such as 'perverts and homosexuals' (these terms were employed as it is by Freud himself in his essay and would nowadays be widely challenged). He observes that these individuals seek their own self as love-object instead of a love-object modelled after their mother. These people, Freud states "are exhibiting a type of object-choice which must be termed 'narcissistic'" (Freud 2013: 22). In the Freudian perspective, primary narcissism is "a positive, libidinal feeling toward the self", and not a perversion. He regards the abandoning of one's primary narcissism and self-love for external love objects as an essential step in the development of the ego, even though he remains vague on when this phase is supposed to take place. Comparing male and female sexes, Freud concludes that "there are fundamental differences between them in respect of their type of object-choice, although these differences are of course not universal" (Freud 2013: 23). Freud notes that object-love of the 'attachment' type or 'anaclitic' type is mainly characteristic of the male; while women, especially if they are good-looking "develop a certain self-contentment which compensates them for the social restrictions that are imposed upon them in their choice of object" (Freud 2013: 25). These women tend to love themselves with an intensity similar to that of the man's love for them. That being said, it is important to mention that Freud does not completely exclude the possibility that some women could love according to the 'anaclitic' type or what he also calls the 'masculine type'. And in the case of narcissistic women who remain indifferent towards men, Freud claims that "in the child which they bear, a part of their own body confronts them like an extraneous object, to which, starting out from their narcissism, they can then give complete object-love" (Freud 2013: 26). Additionally, he acknowledges the case of other women who do not have to wait to become mothers to give complete object-love. These women, even before puberty, feel masculine and develop accordingly along masculine lines. In a nutshell, Freud summarizes his approach to an individual's object-choice as follows:

A person may love: —
(1) According to the narcissistic type:
   a. what he himself is (i.e. himself)
   b. what he himself was,
   c. what he himself would like to be,
   d. someone who was once part of himself.

(2) According to the anaclitic (attachment) type:
   a. the woman who feeds him,
   b. the man who protects him. (Freud 2013: 27)

Although Freud establishes these two groups, he insists that human beings cannot be distinctly divided into those two categories and that both kinds of object-choice are open to each individual, even if he might show a tendency for one more than the other, therefore these categories immediately becomes blurred and confusing. Freud does not only consider the primary narcissism of children but he also examines the attitude of devoted, loving parents towards their children and concludes that "it is the revival and reproduction of their own narcissism, which they have long since abandoned" (Freud 2013: 27). In that case, parents tend to overvalue their offspring, who becomes the centre of the parents' life and are highly considered as "His Majesty the Baby" to use Freud's own term. He explains that the child is expected "to fulfil those wishful dreams of the parents which they never carried out – the boy shall become a great man and a hero in his father's place, and the girl shall marry a prince as a tardy compensation for her mother", and hence, ensure the "immortality of the ego…by taking refuge in the child" (Freud 2013: 28). Freud concludes by stating that "parental love, which is so moving and at the bottom so childish, is nothing but the parents' narcissism born again, which, transformed into object-love, unmistakably reveals its former nature" (ibd.). Even if he acknowledges the importance of primary narcissism in a child's psychological development, he does not address the issue of the disturbances to which a child's original narcissism is exposed; neither does he discuss the defense mechanism the child uses to protect himself from them. Visibly, psychoanalysts unanimously agree on the important contribution of mothers in the infant's physiological and psychological development. Therefore, it is essential to consider the feminist and sociological approach to this issue, which enhances the insight on the representations of motherhood.

2.4 SOCIOLOGICAL AND FEMINIST PERSPECTIVES

In her influential book *The Reproduction of Mothering*, Nancy Chodorow further confirms the important function of 'good mothering', which consists in the mother's ability to make "total environmental provision" (Chodorow 1978: 83) for her infant, that is providing maternal care which will enable her child to deal with his/her anxiety, as well as to cope with his/her environment. Chodorow warns of the consequences that might arise if the mother fails to serve either as an external ego, which then forces the infant to develop prematurely an adaptive ego or on the contrary, if she serves as an adaptive ego for too long. She explains that in these cases "the infant is prevented from developing capacities to deal with anxiety" (ibd.). She emphasizes how crucial it is to differentiate from the mother as well as the other way around and describes the role that a 'good enough mother' plays in the child's development as follows:

> She needs to know both when her child is ready to distance itself and to initiate demands for care, and when it is feeling unable to be distant or separate. This transition can be very difficult because children at this early stage may one minute sense themselves merged with the mother (and require complete anticipatory under-

standing of their needs), and the next, experience themselves as separate and her as dangerous (if she knows their needs in advance). The mother is caught between engaging in "maternal overprotection" (maintaining primary identification and total dependence too long) and engaging in "maternal deprivation" (making premature demands on her infant's instrumentality). (Chodorow 1978: 84)

While in her book, Chodorow seems at first to advocate a change in the sexual division of labour by asking that fathers participate more actively in child rearing, the above passage contradicts her initial intentions by conservatively placing a stringent demand on mothers. Additionally, she remains vague about when this individuation is supposed to take place, although she is convinced of the negative consequences that a prolonged bond between mother and child might entail. Yet, the difficulty that mothers undergo when it comes to separating from their infant stems from their experiencing the child as an extension of themselves. They experience satisfaction from caring for an infant and demonstrate maternal empathy, which derived from total identification with it (see Chodorow 1978: 85). Since mothers consider their child as part of themselves, and strongly empathize with them, they experience the infant's gratification as self-gratification, hence, reciprocating primary love. Chodorow's work is significant in the exploration of the representations of motherhood because in her studies, she considers both the case of infant girls and boys, comparing and contrasting distinctively their relationship with the mother. Because of her lack of empirical evidence to support her hypothesis, Chodorow is forced to base her arguments on object-relation's assumptions to argue that mothers treat daughters differently from sons, which leads mothers to identify with daughters for a longer period of time. She believes that it is through this longer period of identification that daughters develop their relational capacity, which prepares them in turn to become mothers. Therefore, she maintains that this early identification with the mother shapes the difference between masculine and feminine identity, thus perpetuating traditional social roles. Originally, Freud saw oedipal complexes in both genders as completely symmetrical. The boy's oedipal complex consists in his attachment to the mother, an attachment that bears sexual overtones. In this dynamic, the son enters into a triangular conflict, in which the father is seen as a threat, a rival for the mother's love. Accordingly, the son wishes to possess the mother and replace the father. At the same time, he fears castration by his father, hence undergoing a dilemma between his self-love, which results in his narcissistic interest in his penis, and his incestuous love for the mother. As a resolution of his Oedipus complex, the male infant is expected to repress and detach his heterosexual love from his mother and identify with his father, who embodies "the superiority of masculine identification and prerogatives over feminine" (Chodorow 1978: 94). In the case of little girls, at around the age of three, they discover that they have no penis, making them think that they are castrated. They experience their lack as a "narcissistic wound", which is a blow to their self-esteem. Thus, they develop contempt for their mother, who they hold accountable for the missing genital. They seek the penis through their relationship with their father and turn out to hate their mother who they see as a rival, since she has sexual access to the father. When the daughter experiences the mother as a rival and the father as a love object, we talk about the female Oedipus complex, which is "symmetrically opposed to the male Oedipus complex" (Chodorow 1978: 94), but as Chodorow mentions, "heterosexual orientation is thus an oedipal outcome for girls as well as for boys" (Chodorow 1978: 94-95). According to Freud, what mainly differs in a girl's preoedipal relationship with her mother from a boy's is that a girl's phase is much longer than the one of a boy. Both remain attached to the mother sexually but "a boy's relation to his mother soon becomes focused on competitive issues of possession and phallic-sexual oppositeness (or complementarity) to her" (Chodorow 1978: 96). The relation develops into a triangular conflict as a boy considers his father as a rival. A girl, by contrast, remains absorbed for a long time with her mother alone and completely neglects her father. Clearly, there exist differences between the preoedipal mother-daughter and mother-son relationship. Those differences, as the physician and psychoanalyst Robert Fliess demonstrates, can be at best observed through case analysis. In his study, Fliess considers the most recurrent examples of psychopathological extreme and shows that mothers tend to inflict their pathology primarily on daughters. However, he explains that this disparity in the results accounts for the fact that "the picture is more easily recognizable in the female because of the naturally longer duration of the preoedipal phase" (Fliess 1970: 49). In his observations, he considers mothers who were at first 'asymbiotic' during the time their child needed symbiosis and who later became 'hypersymbiotic' when their daughters started to separate themselves from their mothers both mentally and physically. These mothers deny their daughters the individuation they seek and instead treat them as both physical and mental narcissistic extensions of themselves, controlling and using their daughters' sexuality for their own gratification. These mothers engage in what Fliess calls "transitivism of the psychotic" or "I am you and you are me" (Fliess 1970: 48). This results in daughters often reproducing their mothers' psychotic symptoms and their difficulty in developing an individual self. Nonetheless, even if fusion and narcissistic overidentification are predominantly characteristics of mother-daughter relationships, problematic mother-son relationships also exist, but of a different sort. While mothers tend to see their daughters as an extension of their self, boys are experienced as the 'other', even in their symbiotic phase with the mother. Psychoanalysts recognize the social component that shapes the early mother-son relationship. Chodorow explains that "the decline of the husband's presence in the home" has resulted in a wife "as much in need of a husband as the son is of a father", which bears the consequences that "the wife is likely to turn her affection and interest to the next obvious male – her son – and to become particularly seductive toward him" (Chodorow 1978: 104). Again, in such a case, the son is experienced as a sexual other by the mother. The low profile or absence of the father in the household prevents him from countering his wife's seductive behaviour or his son's burgeoning incestuous desires.

In this dynamic, the son depends on the mother "for a sense of self-sufficiency and self-esteem", at the same time "it emphasized these sons' sexuality and sexual difference and encouraged participation in a heavily sexualized relationship in boys who had not resolved early issues of individuation and the establishment of ego boundaries" (Chodorow 1978: 105). In a nutshell, a mother who seeks to fulfil her unmet erotic and emotional needs through her son will treat him as a sexual object, hence reciprocating his incestuous desires and sustaining his infantile dependence. And in the case of the mother-daughter dyad, mothers tend to remain emotionally bound to their daughters, who are experienced as the mothers' double. These daughters eventually develop a poorly individuated sense of self and act as if they are still one with their mother. To Chodorow's examination of the 'good enough mother', Julia Kristeva's work offers an alternative lens to approach the issue of mother-child's individuation, mainly by putting more emphasis on the child's responsibility, rather than the mother's in coming to terms with his/her attachment. In *Black Sun*, Kristeva argues that "matricide is a vital necessity" (Kristeva 1989: 27) in order for the child to grow out of their symbiotic relationship. While she underlines the need for both men and women to murder the mother, she nonetheless stresses that women find it extremely strenuous to come to term with their attachment, for they suffer from what Kristeva designates as "the dead mother complex", reflected through melancholia and depression. However, the child's necessity to symbolically kill the mother in order to grow into an 'independent' individual is subject to controversy and certainly needs to be questioned. While Chodorow seems to offer a more favourable picture of mother-daughter relationships, Kristeva in *Black Sun* appears to suggest a bleaker view of the mother-daughter dyad by providing numerous examples of pathogenic relationships. She insists on the mother's obsessive control over her daughter's subjectivity, which often results in hindering the daughter's use of language as well as her ability to feel. For example, while analysing the French writer Marguerite Duras' writing, Kristeva concludes that images of doubles pervade her work and embody her melancholia. She believes that neither Duras nor her characters succeed in completely freeing themselves from the mother's strong hold. Instead, they turn out to experience a state of affliction from which they never seem to recover. Finally, both Chodorow and Kristeva's work, which draw from object-relations discourse, certainly acknowledge the important role of mothers in the child's development. Yet, they seem to overlook or barely consider the socio-economic, as well as the political condition of women in their analysis, an essential component in the examination of the issue of narcissistic mothers in Modernist literature as the interpretation of the four novels underlines.

2.5 NARCISSISTIC MOTHERS IN MODERNIST NOVELS

Differences between mother-daughter and mother-son relationships exist and need to be considered when examining the question of narcissistic mothers. Accordingly, the novels considered in this book provide both examples of mother-daughter and mother-son relationship. The third chapter of this book focuses on D.H. Lawrence's *Sons and Lovers* (1913), which as the title already indicates, gives an insight into the mother-son relationship. Thus, it concentrates on the character of Gertrude Morel, a narcissistic mother, who undeniably manifests traces of excessive love for her sons William and Paul, preventing them from having a healthy relationship with their father or other women. Even if she shows signs of extreme possessiveness and selfishness, she turns out to be a woman of vision. This constitutes a striking revisionist version of her character. Although she clearly displays signs of narcissism, she still proves to show concern for her sons' happiness. Her incestuous-like love for her son Paul, to some extent, seems to trigger his artistic and creative talents. The ambiguous end of the novel is particularly revealing, as it points at a possible Oedipus complex resolution and the development of Paul as an artist, for as Freud claims: "creativity and suffering are mysteriously allied" (Berman 1990: 37). The fourth chapter examines the mother figures in James Joyce's *Dubliners* (1914). It mainly concentrates on the following short stories: "A Boarding House", "A Mother" and "A Painful Case". In these short stories, Joyce depicts mothers who try to live out their dreams through their daughters but end up being victims of their own ambitions. Joyce invites the reader to consider the social and economic conditions of the time when engaging with these mother figures, hence arousing sympathy for these women, whose narcissism is revealed to be fed and sustained by these factors. Chapter five offers an analysis of Virginia Woolf's novel *To the Lighthouse* (1937) which provides both a representation of mother-daughter and mother-son relationships. Mrs. Ramsay is a narcissistic mother who is in constant need for recognition either from her family or guests for her good deeds and her performance as the perfect hostess and as ideal mother. Many critics have disagreed on whether Mrs. Ramsay should be condemned or praised. This ambivalent attitude stems from Woolf's intention to disrupt the myth of the 'benevolent, selfless mother'. A close reading of this novel shows that this mother's narcissism does not necessarily hinder her maternal ministrations: she is still capable of loving and caring for her children. Her coolness and aloofness, which have been often criticized, are revealed to enable the child's separation from the mother. In this chapter, the relationship between Mrs. Ramsay and James, and the intimacy between Mrs. Ramsay and Lily Briscoe are the centre of attention. Even though Lily is not Mrs. Ramsay's biological child, the connection existing between these two women is very much reminiscent of one between mother and daughter. The key to the examination of Mrs. Ramsay is to be found in Lily's painting. This new reading of the purple triangle discloses Lily's mother issues, in which Mrs. Ramsay becomes the element that contributes to the resolution of the artist's mother-daughter conflict. Finally, Woolf was concerned with the issue of narcissism in connection with violence occasioned by the Great War, suggesting that when narcissism is associated to an excessive sense of ego, the outcome can be fatal. If in this chapter, it is essentially about the violence of World War I, it is nonetheless important to briefly mention the postcolonial readings previously conducted on *To the Lighthouse*. Janet Winston points out that the novel seems to consider "Mr. Ramsay and men and his generation and social class" as responsible for "upholding the world — literally running England and her colonies" (Winston 2009: 68). Thereby, it denounces British imperialism in the world. This issue is reminiscent of Joyce's critique of the Irish case, which resonates through Woolf's character, Mrs. McNab, an Irish working-class woman. She is essential to the writer's critique of what Winston calls "the sustaining colonialism that underpins the English middle-class Victorian family" (Winston 2009: 90). *To the Lighthouse* not only mirrors Woolf's political preoccupations with women's rights, but also the damages of war, imperialism and fascism. Finally, chapter six examines the character of the narcissistic Sasha Jansen from Jean Rhys' novel *Good Morning, Midnight* (1939). Through Sasha, Rhys investigates the role that the mother's ministrations play in the development of the narcissistic self, as well as the consequences it entails on the mother-child relationship. This mother figure is different from the ones in the novels previously examined. The reference to Sasha as a mother is very brief and occurs mainly during her experiencing childbirth, followed by the immediate death of her newborn. Although this episode is succinctly narrated, this scene remains nonetheless highly significant. The child's death should be read as a disruptive element which contributed to Sasha's narcissistic injury, hence reinforcing Sasha's obsession and dependence on commodities, as a way to compensate and mourn the loss of her son. Through her representation of motherhood, Rhys explores how Modernist society encourages and sustains women's narcissistic needs, thus leading them to take actively part in mass consumption. Yet, the novel offers a positive valuation of consumerism, by underlining the liberating aspect of make-up, fashion and alcohol for Sasha, who turns out to be reclaiming the city streets. In the light of Walter Benjamin's theory of the 'flâneur', Sasha's role of the "unwilling detective" (Benjamin 2006: 72) investigating consumer society is put forward. At last, Rhys' criticism of narcissism develops into a political discourse by suggesting how narcissism can become a means to resist the nationalist discourse of the time. All in all, these Modernist novels present different types of narcissistic mothers. Gertrude Morel is an overwhelming mother who fosters her son's narcissistic personality, which turns out to develop his artistic faculties; while the mothers in *Dubliners*, who try to live out their dream through their daughters also demonstrate the extent to which their actions are controlled by socio-economic pressures. Virginia Woolf's narcissistic mother (Mrs. Ramsay) appears to lack empathy but her emotional detachment allows her children to separate and develop their own sense of self. Sasha's narcissistic scar appears to be the result of a traumatic experience, namely the death of her infant, which pushes her to find reparative measures through consumerism. The range of texts covered in this book – from working-class Midlands, Irish Catholic, Victorian-Edwardian intelligentsia to post-colonial cosmopolitan – show that narcissism inevitably involve socio-economic components and has a collected dimension. These Modernist writers demonstrate that it is essential to consider the interaction of social and economic factors before condemning these self-absorbed mothers, for Western individualistic society seems to advocate the romanticized but erroneous image of 'perfect mother', while at the same time fostering their narcissistic behaviour. If Modernist literature provides countless examples of narcissistic mothers, this issue is not specific to 20th century Western society; it continues to this day to draw attention and generates discussions, for instance with the recent controversy surrounding the social development of 'Tiger Mother' in Chinese culture and the concept of 'Kyōiku Mama' in modern Japanese society, which refer to a harsh and demanding mother, who pushes her children to climb the social ladder through rigorous education and competition.

3 A Mother's Vision and Love in D.H. Lawrence's *Sons and Lovers*

Over the course of his career as novelist, playwright, poet, essayist, literary critic and painter, D.H. Lawrence was well-known for causing a stir among literary critics, who were often scandalized by the explicit sexuality in his works. Therefore, few are those who would have expected the author of famous erotic novels and obscene paintings to be considered a significant writer on family relationships. Yet, a closer look at Lawrence's works reveals that most of them have something to say about parenthood, especially motherhood, and childhood, for instance, his painting "A Holy Family" (see *D.H. Lawrence's Paintings* 23) projects the image of a happy nuclear family, composed of the father, "a moustachioed man in a bright blue shirt who resembles Lawrence himself, embracing his blonde, bare-breasted consort" (Graham-Dixon 2003: 3). On the left-hand side corner of the picture, a child, who positioned slightly at the back, contemplates blissfully the harmony that prevails in the household. The yellow halos on the parents' head are reminiscent of the ring of light often used in religious iconography to symbolize the holiness of the depicted figures. At the same time, they are here presumably used, Andrew Graham-Dixon notes, "to signify the sacredness of the sexual act [...], a conviction that runs like a leitmotiv through all of his novels, essays and letters of the writer's later years" (Graham-Dixon 2003: 3). But, if at first the portrait evokes the idea of an ideal family, the presence of the phallus in the picture provides an alternative interpretation to the image of a happy family. In his letter to a friend, Lawrence admits that he "put a phallus in each one of my pictures somewhere. And I paint no picture that won't shock people's castrated social spirituality" (Lawrence 1989: 648). The illustration of the phallus in "A Holy Family" is a reference to the Oedipus complex. Its position, in the background, symbolizes the son's desire to be sexually involved with his mother, a thought further reinforced by the child enviously watching his father as he is holding his wife's naked body. The mother's naked breast possibly suggests her son's need to be nurtured, as well as his incestuous longing for her and thereby, his desire to kill the father. These motives can be found in many of Lawrence's novels of the middle period, for example in *Sons and Lovers* (1913), *The Rainbow* (1915), and *Women in Love* (1920) along with his exploration of bad marriages and adulterous relationships. The representation of Paul Morel's Oedipus complex in *Sons and Lovers* and James Ramsay's in Virginia Woolf's *To the Lighthouse* is significant in the approach to the question of narcissistic mothers in Modernist literature. Simultaneously, it is a reminder of Sigmund Freud's influence on these authors. Indeed, in *Fantasia of the Unconscious* (1922), Lawrence confirms being familiar with the Freudian psychoanalytic discourse, which justifies the examination of his novel, especially the mother-son relationship, from a Freudian perspective. He declares that "we are bound to admit that into all human relationships, particularly adult human relationships, a large element of sex enters. We are thankful that Freud has insisted on this" (Lawrence 1930: 13). He further adds that he believes that "what Freud says is always partly true" (ibd.). If Lawrence was surely influenced by Freud's psychanalytic theories, he nevertheless detested Alfred Booth Kuttner's Oedipal reading of Paul Morel's relationship with his mother. In his letter to Barbara Low, a pioneer of analytic theory in England, he protests: "I hated the Psychoanalytic Review of *Sons and Lovers* [...] My poor book: it was, as art, a fairly complete truth: so, they carve a half lie out of it, and say 'Voilà.' Swine!" (Lawrence 1982: 655). Lawrence's rejection of Kuttner's interpretation should not be taken as his dismissal of psychoanalysis. In fact, the writer developed his own ideas of family relationships, for example in his essay "Education of the People" (1925), in which he condemns the mother's stifling love and concludes that "there should be a league for the prevention of maternal love, as there is a society for the prevention of cruelty to animals" (Lawrence 1988: 121). If in *Education of the People*, Lawrence mainly addresses the issue of maternal domination, in *Fantasia of the Unconscious*, he discusses the role the father should play in the child's personal development. Judith Ruderman observes that in Lawrence's view "in order to develop healthily, the child needs a father to counteract the smothering, stultifying effects of the mother's characteristic means of parenting, by spanking the child to activate its ganglia and helping the move toward independence" (Ruderman 1984: 32). Therefore, it is in the light of Lawrence's own observations of the family that the analysis of Gertrude Morel is conducted in this chapter. She is revealed to manifest traces of excessive love for her sons, William and Paul, preventing them from leading a healthy relationship, either with their father or with other women. Her disproportionate affection and the consequences it entails on both sons have gained her the reputation of "devouring mother", to use Ruderman's coinage, and to be seen as an antagonist to her children's psychological well-being. However, although this obsessive mother displays signs of self-centeredness, she also turns out to be passionately human. Deeply in love with William and later on with Paul, she shows on several occasions that she still wishes them well, envisioning for them an ambitious future. So, Lawrence's depiction of this excessive mother, who tries to find reparation for her narcissistic injury through her exclusive love for her sons, outgrows the negative image that one might get of her, instead making room for a somehow more indulgent judgment of this narcissistic mother, and then at the end, he even exonerates her. At last, it turns out that these notions of passion, excess and vision, perhaps against all expectations, are in fact incarnated through the character of Mrs. Morel.

3.1 MRS. MOREL'S NARCISSISTIC INJURY

Starting his narrative with a section describing 'the early married life of the Morels' (as stated by the title itself), Lawrence emphasizes Gertrude and Walter's initial meeting, followed by the failure of their marriage, which constitutes the primary source of the conflict at the centre of the novel. This opening chapter is crucial in casting light on the source of Gertrude's potential narcissistic injury and in revealing her self-absorption. Significantly, the novel begins with a detailed description of Mrs. Morel's, previously Gertrude Coppard, upbringing in a 'good old burgher family' (Lawrence 1992: 15) that has gone bankrupt. Lawrence insists that she inherited her temper, her pride, and her rigidity from her father, George Coppard, and stresses the complicated relationship existing between father and daughter. It is pointed out that Gertrude's personality has been influenced by the strict, puritan education she received as a child. At the same time, the reader's attention is drawn to Gertrude's sense of pride and subtle beauty:

> In her person she was rather small and delicate, with a large brow, and dropping bunches of brown silk curls. She had the beautiful hands of the Coppards. Her dress was always subdued. She wore dark blue silk, with a peculiar silver chain of silver scallops. This, and a heavy brooch of twisted gold, was her only ornament. She was still perfectly intact, deeply religious, and full of beautiful candour. (Lawrence 1992: 17)

Here, Mrs. Morel's natural beauty, as well as her remarkable inclination for precious materials such as silk, silver and gold, are brought to the attention of the reader, thus alluding to her exquisite and sophisticated taste and further suggesting that pride and keeping up appearances constitute two essential features of her character. The effects of her lady-like demeanour as well as her narcissism are reinforced when she remembers "to have been petted and flattered by all the men when she had gone on the dockyard, for she was a rather proud child" (Lawrence

1992: 16). The hyperbolic use of the adjective "all" in "all the men" signals the character's excessive feeling of self-importance, which is further confirmed by the statement that "she was rather proud", which concludes the narrator's remarks. These personality traits prove to be first an asset but also rapidly, the source of her misery. When Walter Morel encounters Gertrude Coppard for the first time at a Christmas party, he is immediately attracted to Gertrude's elegance and "seemed melted away before her" (Lawrence 1992: 17). Then the reader is told that "she was to the miner that thing of mystery and fascination, a lady. When he spoke to him, it was with a southern pronunciation and a purity of English which thrilled him to hear" (ibd.). As for Gertrude, watching Walter, she first notices him in sexualized terms, as "well set-up, erect, and very smart" (Lawrence 1992: 17), then in financial terms, indicated through the double meaning of "well set-up", which as Macdonald Daly points out, shows that "Walter gives the impression of a man who has good material prospects" (Daly 2005: 82). This belief is then reinforced by Gertrude's observation that he "wore the ribbon of the teetotaller" (Lawrence 1992: 19), "an outward sign of a sober mind and, in all likelihood, equally sober finances" (Daly 2005: 82). While she is seduced by Morel's exuberance and sensuality, she also immediately realizes that the miner is the antipode of her austere father, whose humour was "satiric" (Lawrence 1992: 18). George Coppard, the reader is told, was a man who "ignored all sensuous pleasure" and was "proud in his bearing, handsome, and rather bitter" (ibd.). Gertrude's fascination with Walter stems from her recognizing in this relationship the possibility to defy her father's authority and finally rebel against the austerity she grew up with. However, rapidly the reader realizes that Gertrude and Walter do not have much in common, and that they are a rather incongruous match. While Walter is portrayed as being "soft" and "non-intellectual", Gertrude is said to have "a curious, receptive mind", "clever in leading other folk on to talk" and "was considered very intellectual" (Lawrence 1992: 17). Accordingly, from the beginning, it seems that their union is set up for failure. Barbara Schapiro confirms that "Gertrude was originally attracted by Walter because he represented precisely what she (and her father) lacked – spontaneous, emotional, and sensual expressiveness" (Schapiro 1999: 154). However, as Lawrence realizes "another person can never complete or fill the void in the self. Selves can only balance and complement one another. The empty or fractured self may typically seek to absorb or devour the other in an attempt to compensate for the deficiency" (ibd.). This is illustrated through Gertrude's restless attempts to turn Walter into someone he is not, a behaviour which only contribute to arousing hostility in the couple. Macdonald Daly explains that: "what ruins it decisively is Walter Morel's inability to deliver to Gertrude the bourgeois material standards she has been led to expect their marriage to secure" (Daly 2005: 82). Then, shortly after being married to Walter, she discovers with intense disappointment that he may have embellished the truth concerning his social status: Walter does not own any houses as he claims he does but in fact pays rent to his mother, and still owes money for their furniture. Rapidly, Mrs. Morel grows more and more into a displeased wife, a feeling worsened by her complete isolation when she moves to the Bottoms. As the name 'Bottoms' ironically suggests, her desire and hope for social ascension are at once shattered, leaving her with an excruciating feeling of disappointment and weariness, for "she was sick of it, the struggle with poverty and ugliness and meanness" (Lawrence 1992: 13). In fact, in relative terms, their standard of living was quite good, and all the children had access to higher education. However, her misjudgement, accountable for her bad choices in life, is responsible for her discontentment and represents a blow to her narcissistic pride, and by extension to her ego. The omniscient narrative voice confirms that after she finds out about her husband's lies, "Gertrude sat white and silent. She was her father now ... She said very little to her husband, but her manner had changed towards him. Something in her proud, honorable soul had crystallized out hard as a rock" (Lawrence 1992: 21). Mrs. Morel's "crystallized soul" is the symbolic illustration of an individual who is narcissistically wounded. As a result, she seeks reparative measures in order to make up for her feeling of humiliation and shame. First, she tries to radically change her husband, in order for him to meet her high expectations, however, as the reader learns: "the pity was, she was too much of his opposite. She could not be content with the little he might be, she would have him the much that he ought to be" (Lawrence 1992: 25). By forcing him into someone he is not, or as the narrator puts it "in seeking to make him nobler than he could be, she destroyed him" (ibd.). The narrator's conclusion that "she injured and hurt and scarred herself, but she lost none of her worth" (ibd.) indicates that as much as Walter is to be blamed for his wife's displeasure, she nonetheless also equally has her share of responsibility. Also, the statement that "she lost none of her worth", then immediately followed by the narrator's remark "she also had the children" (ibd.), reasserts her determination in seeking further reparation for her narcissistic wound, this time through her claustrophobic relationship with her sons, first William, then Paul. Gămini Salgădo agrees that "it is partly the economic deprivation perpetually confronting her which forces Mrs. Morel to seek her fulfilment in the over-possessiveness towards her sons" (Salgădo 1996: 10). Schapiro explains that "as a woman, her option for self-realization and expression are limited to her role as mother and to a vicarious experience of achievement through the lives of her sons" (Schapiro 1999: 152).

3.2 MRS. MOREL'S WOUNDED NARCISSISM

3.2.1 Mrs. Morel's Exclusive Love for William

Focusing on mothers who are themselves in need of narcissistic supplies, Alice Miller concludes that these mothers seek to satisfy their own narcissistic needs through their child. However, she argues that "this does not rule out strong affection" (Morrison 1986: 326). In fact quite the opposite: "the mother often loves her child as her self-object passionately, but not in the way he needs to be loved ... instead, he develops something the mother needs, and which certainly saves his life (the mother's love) at the time, but nevertheless may prevent him, throughout his life, from being himself" (ibd.). This pattern is first illustrated through Mrs. Morel's relationship with her eldest son, William and later on with Paul. Unable to establish a stable and satisfying relationship with her husband, even if as the reader is told "there were many, many stages in the ebbing of her love for him" (Lawrence 1992: 62), which implies the existence of passion in their relationship, Gertrude tries to make up for her dissatisfaction through her exclusive bond with William, whose birth, "came just when her own bitterness of disillusion was hardest to bear; when her faith in life was shaken, and her soul felt dreary and lonely" (Lawrence 1992: 22). As her love for William grows, the more she despises her husband, and consequently "turned to the child" and "turned from the father" (ibd.). Slowly, it is revealed that a symbiotic relationship exists between mother and son, primarily visible in the episode of the wakes, which is reported from William's point of view. First, the reader is told that the young boy would listen to his mother "as if spellbound" (Lawrence 1992: 12), a word which emphasizes Mrs. Morel's mesmerizing power and authority on her son. Then the narrator describes William's attachment to his mother as follows "he would not leave her. All the time he stuck close to her, bristling with a small boy's pride of her" (ibd.). This reference to the "boy's pride" reminds the reader of the Coppard's sense of pride which both Gertrude and her father possess. Through the narrator's comment that "no other woman looked such a lady as she did" (ibd.), the reader gets direct access to William's consciousness in his assessment of his mother, which casts doubts on the objectivity of the observation. William's fascination with his mother's physical appearance is one of the multiple allusions to the incestuous nature of their love for each other, a thought further accentuated by the image of William "cut to the heart", "when she went slowly away with her little girl, whilst her son stood watching her", leaving him "miserable" (Lawrence 1992: 12) and unable to enjoy the wakes without her. Being trapped in this symbiotic relation with his mother, he experiences her absence as a painful void, preventing him from having a pleasant time once she is gone. Yet, this description and particularly these phrases "he would not leave her" and "...he stuck close to her", Carol Sklenicka notes, also present a "complex mosaic of perspectives" through the shift in the apparently omniscient point of view, which not only contributes to conveying William's consciousness but intentionally "represents the mother's sensibility", and denotes "a pridefully possessive maternal attitude" (Sklenicka 1991: 41). This interdependence between mother and son is reiterated later on in the novel, first through William's constant need, even as a young adult, to come back to her, for instance, William refuses to seize the opportunity of going on a trip to the Mediterranean and instead "came home for his fortnight's holiday" (Lawrence 1992: 107). The narrator remarks that "not even the Mediterranean, which pulled at all his young man's desire to travel, and at his poor man's wonder at the glamorous south could take him away when he might come home. That compensated his mother for much" (ibd.). Then later on through the description of Gertrude's excruciating pain at the thought of William moving to London, the strong bond between them is again emphasized. Subject to the strain imposed by the distance which separates them, Gertrude Morel opts for an epistolary correspondence hoping to bridge this geographical and emotional gap. The reader learns that she "wrote him every week", "thought of him all day long" and that in her eyes "he was like her knight who wore her favour in the battle" (Lawrence 1992: 103). This scene is marked with romantic undertones, reminiscent of the fin' Amor tradition, a medieval literary conception of love that emphasizes chivalry and bears the connotation of something illicit but at the same time morally elevating. Thus, William endorses the role of a lover. However, as the novel progresses it is revealed that Mrs. Morel does not only seek emotional fulfilment through her tight relationship with her eldest son, but this latter turns out to act more like a husband or a lover. This is visible when one evening, at the sight of his mother's "swollen and discoloured eyes" (Lawrence 1992: 83), William almost engages in a fist fight with his father. This scene, in particular, unravels many aspects of the family ties. First, the children's aversion to their father is made evident through the use of the determiner "all" in "*all* the children...were peculiarly against their father, along with their mother" (*my emphasis*; Lawrence 1992: 83), justified by the reference to Walter's uncontrolled anger and aggression towards his wife. Then, in the following: "There was a silence as William was white to the lips, and his fists were clenched. He waited until the children were silent [...]; then he said: 'you coward, you daren't do it when I was in'" (ibd.), William stands out from the children category. A well-defined line is drawn between the adults' faction, to which William belongs, and the children's group. This clear separation between William and his siblings purposely insists on the incestuous nature of the love between mother and son, pointing at William's unconscious desire to fight his father in order to take over the position of head of the family. At the same time, if we think of William as an adult, the confrontation between these two men takes the form of a fight to win over the heart of their beloved. This idea of incestuous love is later reiterated when Gertrude overtly demonstrates excessive possessiveness and jealousy when she feels her relationship with William is threatened by other women, for example she does not hesitate to turn her son's sweethearts away when they come to the house, looking for him. Finally, when she receives a letter with the photograph of Gipsy, her son's girlfriend from London, she cannot help sneering at the way the young lady dresses and with disdain she wonders if Gipsy "ever wears anything except evening clothes" (Lawrence 1992: 127). Responding to his mother's sarcasm, Paul concedes that she is a little too harsh and perhaps also unfair to the girl: "'you are disagreeable mother,'... 'I think the first one with the bare shoulders is lovely'" (ibd.). But slowly, Mrs. Morel succeeds in playing off the other members of the family against the young girl, whose shallowness and lack of consideration for others surely further contribute in making her unpopular. William himself, at time, resents Gipsy for her overbearing attitude towards his sister, Annie, for instance when she requests to have her clothes washed: "'Oh, would you mind,' she said to Annie, 'washing me these two blouses, and these things?'" (Lawrence 1992: 159). This demand infuriates both Mrs. Morel and William. The reference to Gipsy's superficiality and simple-mindedness contributes to adding a layer of complexity to Gertrude Morel's portrayal as possessive, suffocating mother. From the tight connection existing between William and Gertrude, it is made clear that William's exclusive affection for his mother certainly makes up for her lack of self-esteem. Not only does he bring emotional support to his mother's wounded narcissism, but he allows her to live out her dreams of social aspirations through him, hence "making the world glow again for her" (Lawrence 1992: 63). Mrs. Morel plays an active part in facilitating her son's contribution to soothing her narcissistic injury by directing the course of his future and insisting on his education. Confronting her husband, she says authoritatively of William: "He is not going in the pit" (Lawrence 1992: 70) and she makes sure that her son finds a white-collar job, which slowly enables him to play the role which according to Gertrude, Walter failed to fulfil, that of breadwinner. By deciding on, as well as influencing, her son's future, Mrs. Morel takes possession of William, which as Macdonald Daly explains: "William's rise to the lower middle class, aged twenty, is marred by the equation of financial reward with emotional attachment" (Daly 2005: 84), which is expressed when William declares to his mother "And I can give you twenty pounds a year, Mater – we s'll all be rolling in money" (Lawrence 1992: 78). William's previous statement indicates the role money plays in tightening the affective maternal bond. Gămini Salgădo confirms the existence of a strong interconnection between emotional and financial ties. He explains that "the breaking of the economic ties is symptomatic of the loosening of emotional ones" (Salgădo 1996: 21), a statement which is illustrated first through Gertrude's detachment from her husband once she realizes that he is unable to offer her the bourgeois standard of living she longs for, then again through the transference of her incestuous love to her second son, Paul, which takes effect as soon as William fails to send her money as he promised he would. Finally, William's tragic death is announced at the end of part I, marking the "complete transference from William to Paul" (Salgădo 1996: 25). This is best summed up by the narrator's comment that "Mrs Morel's life now rooted itself in Paul" (Lawrence 1992: 171).

3.2.2 Mrs. Morel's Constraining Love for Paul

Mrs. Morel's narcissistic attachment to Paul, at first sight, appears to be a major turnaround in the novel, since "she did not want it" and felt like "this coming child was too much for her" (Lawrence 1992: 13). This feeling is again reiterated in another key passage, which occurs shortly after Paul's birth and is told mainly through psycho-narration. Thereby, it grants direct access to Mrs. Morel's thoughts:

> *The baby* was restless on *his* mother's knee, clambering with his hands at the light.
> Mrs Morel looked down at *him*. She had dreaded *this baby* like a catastrophe, because of her feeling for her husband. And now she felt strangely towards *the infant*. Her heart was heavy because of *the child*, almost as if it were unhealthy, or malformed. Yet *it* seemed quite well. But she noticed the peculiar knitting of *the baby*'s brows, and the peculiar heaviness of *its* eyes, as if *it* were trying to understand something that was pain. She felt, when she looked at *the child*'s dark, brooding pupils, as if a burden were on her heart […]
> In her arms lay *the delicate baby*. *Its* deep, blue eyes; always looking up at her unblinking, seemed to draw her innermost thoughts out of her. She no longer loved her husband; she had not wanted *this child* to come, and there *it* lay in her arms and pulled at her heart. She felt as if the navel string that had connected *its* frail little body with hers had not been broken. A wave of hot love went over her to *the infant*. She held *it* close to her face and breast. With all her force, with all her soul she would make up to *it* for having brought *it* into the world unloved. She would love *it* all the more now *it* was here; carry it in her love. *Its* clear, knowing eyes gave her pain and fear. Did *it* know all about her? When

it lay under her heart, had *it* been listening then? Was there a reproach in the look? She felt the marrow melt in her bones, with fear and pain. (*my emphasis*; Lawrence 1992: 50-51)

Here, it is important to note the alternated use of the two different third-person pronouns ('he' and 'it') to refer to baby Paul, which according to Violeta Sotirova is "rather unusual, especially since the alternations happen to occur in close proximity" (Sotirova 2011: 65). Sotirova points out that in this passage, the baby is predominantly referred to as 'it' and only a few times as 'he', which "would seem startling in view of semantic value of *it* as a personal pronoun" (Sotirova 2011: 66), since the pronoun 'it' is commonly used to refer to inanimate objects or animals. The variation from the use of 'he' to the impersonal pronoun 'it' in referring to the baby appears to be connected to the author's intention in suggesting the possible estrangement between mother and child. Sotirova observes that "the first occurrence of *his* at the beginning of the passage is in a sentence markedly narratorial" (Sotirova 2011: 68), aiming at primarily describing an action, and same applies to 'him' in "Mrs Morel looked down at *him*", which describes, from an external perspective, Mrs. Morel's action. However, Sotirova informs us when a pronoun is finally used in rendering Mrs. Morel's thoughts on the baby, it turns out that it is the third-person neuter 'it' which is favoured. More than just being a stylistic variation, the alternate use of the third person pronouns in this passage aims at emphasizing Gertrude's feeling of disappointment with her husband, which serves as justification for her not wanting the baby. It also shows the internal conflict she undergoes. While the neuter 'it' first seems to indicate Mrs. Morel's feeling of estrangement from her child, as the narrative progresses, it exposes this mother's guilt and self-reproach, and consequently, it also prefigures her possessive attachment to Paul. Violeta Sotirova confirms that "this switch from *it* to *he* in Mrs Morel's inner discourse can probably be explained semantically with the emotional shift that takes place in her: from being cold and alienated at first from the baby ... to growing more positive" (Sotirova 2011: 73).

It is interesting to compare the references to Paul and his siblings in the text. Sotirova remarks that while baby Paul, as shown earlier, is extensively referred to as 'it' in the narration, the two other sons, William and Arthur, are designated as 'he' from the start, as indicated below first through William's portrayal:

> The boy was small and frail at first, but *he* came on quickly. *He* was a beautiful child, with dark gold ringlets, and dark-blue eyes which changed gradually to a clear grey. *His* mother loved him passionately. *He* came just when her own bitterness of disillusion was hardest to bear; when her faith in life was shaken, and her soul felt dreary and lonely. She made much of the child and the father was jealous. (*my emphasis*; Lawrence 1992: 22)

then, through the description of the newborn Arthur:

> They called the baby Arthur. *He* was very pretty, with a mop of gold curls, and *he* loved his father from the first. Mrs Morel was glad this child loved the father. Hearing the miner's footsteps, the baby would put up *his* arms and crow. (*my emphasis*; Lawrence 1992: 64)

Yet, while the use of 'it' has been associated with the unemotional and the distant, it seems that in the text, its use is very ambiguous. As mentioned earlier, the neuter 'it' generally refers to an inanimate object or an animal, rather than to an individual. However, in *Sons and Lovers*, Gertrude's reference to her son as 'it', is revealed to insist on this mother's view of her son as an object of possession. Thus, it underlines Mrs. Morel's excessive attachment to Paul, which seems to be stronger and more obsessive than her bond with William. This thought is further emphasized when the reader is told that "Mrs Morel's intimacy with her second son was more subtle and fine, perhaps not so passionate as with her eldest" (Lawrence 1992: 93). Moreover, the reference to the unbroken "navel string that had connected its frail little body with hers" (Lawrence 1992: 51) confirms the exclusivity of their relationship, predicting an identity confusion, which is reinforced by Paul's physical description. He is said to be "built like his mother" (Lawrence 1992: 82) and emotionally, he was very conscious of how his mother felt, so that "when she fretted he understood, and could have no peace. His soul seemed always attentive to her" (ibd.). Therefore, it is obvious that between mother and child exists a physical, as well as a psychic connection, which contributes to the thought of Paul as an extension of Mrs. Morel's narcissistic self. The exclusive synergy of the connection between them, which is absent in her relationship with William, is further illustrated when Mr. Morel, losing his temper, throws a drawer at his wife and accidently cuts her left brow, which "was bleeding rather profusely" (Lawrence 1992: 53). The reader is told that Mrs. Morel "glanced down at the child, her brain reeling, some drops of blood soaked into its white shawl; but the baby was at least not hurt" (ibd.). This scene evokes the performance of a blood ritual, featuring Gertrude and Paul, who intermingling their blood seem to grow stronger as one. This statement is reinforced by Walter's thought following his observation of the blood "soak[ing] through the baby's scalp", that "finally, his manhood broke" (Lawrence 1992: 77). Here, the mother and child's fusion is epitomized, but not without consequences, for "baptized by his father in his mother's blood, the baby Paul becomes his mother's child, and his father's emasculator" (Sklenicka 1991: 54). Later on, Paul's complete rejection of Walter is suggested on many occasions by his wish to see his father dead, for after all, "his ambition, as far as this world's gear went, was quietly to earn his thirty-five shillings a week somewhere near home, and then, when his father died, have a cottage with his mother, paint and go out as he liked, and live happy ever after" (Lawrence 1992: 114). Paul expresses strong desires to replace his father and take over the role of head of the family. Raking the fire, he proudly declares to his mother: "I'm the man in the house now" (Lawrence 1992: 113). This desire to replace the father sheds light on Paul's Oedipal complex and is accentuated by the large amount of instances in the novel which indicate his incestuous love for Mrs. Morel, with whom he "loved to sleep" (Lawrence 1992: 92), and to whom he "could not bear to go home...empty" (Lawrence 1992: 93) for fear of disappointing her. He would rather fish out a little spray and bring it to her as a manifestation of his affection, which she will accept as "a love-token" (ibd.). He does not spare on compliments to his mother. Dazzled by Mrs. Morel's appearance, he makes sure to let her know how wonderful she looks in her new cotton blouse (Lawrence 1992: 151). Yet, Paul seems to be unable to overcome his Oedipal complex contrarily to other children. For that, Alfred Kuttner argues that if Gertrude Morel is to be blamed for her narcissistic love for Paul, which contributes to reinforcing the child's attachment to her, Walter Morel equally shares responsibility for his son's inability to get over his fixation upon the mother. He explains that Paul occupies an "unnatural position in the family" and this "is responsible for the distortion of the normal attitude of the child towards its parents" (Kuttner 1985: 5). He adds that "the father ideal simply does not exist for Paul [...] the child's normal dependence upon the mother is perpetuated because there is no counter-influence to detach it from her" (ibd.). As a result, their love for one another appears to be an exclusive one, as "Mrs Morel clung now to Paul" (Lawrence 1992: 142) and so did he to her. Paul becomes his mother's confidant and they hold no secrets from each other: "the two shared lives" (ibd.), until he meets Miriam. Slowly, Mrs. Morel feels that her relationship with Paul is jeopardized by her son's drawing nearer to the young girl. She reacts by showing intense jealousy and attempts to undermine her rival. Determined she claims: "she would fight to keep Paul" (Lawrence 1992: 262). When Paul starts seeing Miriam, Mrs. Morel adopts a defensive attitude. She immediately feels the potential threat that the young girl represents to her exclusive relationship with Paul. While Gertrude considers Miriam a substantial opponent, she does not think of Clara as a potential threat and believes that Paul "will tire of her" (Lawrence 1992: 374). Comparing her behaviour towards William and her attitude towards Paul, it becomes noticeable that her possession over William occurs mainly in an economic scope. She cannot accept losing her financial privileges to the benefit of her son's bourgeois girlfriend, for she still takes credit for William's success and upward mobility. As for Paul, her desire to keep her son exclusively to herself is triggered by her incapacity to detach from him, and to see him as other, a feeling accentuated and sustained by Paul's constant demand for his mother's care. His longing for her attention encourages Gertrude's narcissism, at the same time as it reinforces Paul's Oedipal complex.

3.3 A WOMAN OF VISION

Even if Mrs. Morel in seeking reparation for her narcissistic injury attempts to assuage her emotional emptiness through her excessive affection for her sons, she still proves to be a woman of vision. After all these two terms 'narcissism' and 'vision' can often be seen as complementary. Being constantly on the lookout for opportunities for self-enhancement, narcissists are able to project themselves ahead, so as to be able to assess the potential impact and repercussions of their acts. Mrs. Morel is capable of recognizing opportunities for social ascension through her children just like Mrs. Kearney and Mrs. Mooney in James Joyce's *Dubliners* seek fast upward mobility through their daughters Kathleen and Polly. Although Mrs. Morel similarly uses her sons' success to cross a class boundary, she nonetheless demonstrates that she wishes for her children what she long wished for herself: an upward journey into the bourgeoisie and greater material security. Aware of William's intelligence, she encourages him to pursue his education in the prospect of finding a 'decent' job. Contrarily to her husband, she is convinced of the negative aspects of mining employment and makes sure that her children would not end up in the pit like their father. Taking initiatives, when William was thirteen, "she got him a job in the 'Co-op' office" (Lawrence 1992: 69) as a means to facilitate his *début* on the job market. Not even the confrontation she has with Walter (see Lawrence 1992: 70) could lessen her determination and hope to see her children succeed professionally. Their conversation, which is told through the use of reported direct speech, emphasizes the social and cultural gap existing between Gertrude and Walter. Simultaneously, it underlines Mrs. Morel's superiority over her husband, first in the different language register they use to communicate with one another, then by signalling Gertrude's ability to project herself in the future, while her husband on the contrary clearly demonstrates his lack of foresight. Gertrude does not only contrast with her husband for believing that education is key to social mobility, but also in her attempt to challenge women's domestic role. The text briefly suggests her commitment to the advancement of woman's rights through her adherence to the Women's Guild, which urges its members to question "the conditions of their own lives and find faults" (Lawrence 1992: 69). Her involvement in the promotion of women's rights, once again confirms her ability to detect opportunity for self-enhancement, as well as to seize chances to serve her own interests, for instance in obtaining more freedom for herself and fellow women. When it comes to Paul, Mrs. Morel was confident that "Paul was going to distinguish himself. She had a great belief in him, the more because he was unaware of his own powers" (Lawrence 1992: 222). This assertion insists on her motherly pride and faith in her son's future success. Then infiltrating Gertrude's mind, the narration stresses this mother's vision of a brighter future, which is revealed to be primarily spurred by her own desires for upward mobility. This idea is underlined by her conclusion that "life for her was rich with promise" and that "she was to see herself fulfilled" (ibd.). In this scene, the mother's self-centeredness is reiterated. If at first, she refers to her son's achievement and her pride in him, at the end, it becomes evident that she is praising herself, acknowledging her personal contributions to her son's success, which once again serves as reparation for her injured narcissism as the switch in the use of pronouns suggests. The substitution of the pronoun 'he' for 'she' indicates a change of direction in Mrs. Morel's thoughts, from at first concentrating on Paul, they end up converging toward her own 'self', showing that she does not lose focus on her own interest. Strikingly, Paul sees it from a different perspective. For him, he is the one "who had done something for her, if only a trifle. All his works was hers" (Lawrence 1992: 222). His attitude is reminiscent of Alice Miller's claim that the child develops something the mother needs in order to maintain her affection. Gertrude invests time and effort in securing her son's future, and at the same time, her own. She is the one who arranged the job at 'Thomas Jordan and Son', a small company specializing in surgical appliances. Her eagerness in helping Paul find a job reveals that she has her son's best interest at heart as long as it can also serve her own need. Yet, her involvement and enthusiasm in obtaining a job interview for Paul is revealed to further tighten the bond uniting mother and son. Paul's dependence on his mother is blatant, as well as his admiration for her. Escorted by his mother to his interview, the reader learns that Paul "was sensible all the time of having her opposite of him" (Lawrence 1992: 117). From their eye contact, the complicity between Mrs. Morel and her son is accentuated. The metaphorical phrase, "then each looked out of the window" (ibd.) is an indication of the protagonists' ability to project themselves into the future, sharing similar thoughts and again reinforcing the contrast with Walter. By influencing her children's career choices, Mrs. Morel raises them according to her own expectations, which has the consequences of making both William and Paul feel superior to their father and show resentment to the mining community. Since both William and Paul have a 'white-collar' job, they often feel superior to their father and show resentment to the mining community. This is mainly conveyed through Paul's condescension for Mr. Braithwaite and Mr. Winterbottom's grammar mistakes, of which he tells his mother "They're hateful, and common, and hateful, they are, and I'm not going any more. Mr Braithwaite drops his "h's", and Mr Winterbottom says "You was" (Lawrence 1992: 97). This episode illustrates the importance of language in social ascension but also in reinforcing the sons' attachment to their mother which in turn also exacerbates their estrangement from their father. Although Gertrude's ambition for her children contributed to reinforcing their alienation from their father, can she really be condemned for preventing her children to end up in the pits, whose perilous features have been brought to attention through the numerous realist descriptions that pervade the narration?

If Gertrude appears to be concerned about her sons' future, her ability to project herself is not limited to the professional side, as she proves to be capable of reading into human relationships. Gertrude's disapproval of her sons' girlfriends partly stems from her "jealousy, her fear of losing the two sons in whom she had placed all her love" (Black 2005: 64), but also reflects her clever perception of the incongruous match that William and Gipsy, then later Paul and Miriam represent. When William confesses of his first girlfriends that he is only looking for "a bit of fun" (Black 2005: 64) and that "when they've done, I trot away", Gertrude warns him that "one day you'll find a string around your neck" (Lawrence 1992: 80). This oracle-like statement is proven to be confirmed later when William admits repeatedly to his mother that although he is aware of Gipsy's shallowness and foolishness, he has "gone too far to break off now" (Lawrence 1992: 161), hence resulting in him overworking in order to "make some money to marry on" (Lawrence 1992: 165). As for Paul, while she accepts the affair between Clara and him, she strongly disapproves of his relationship with Miriam, who she believes is "not like an ordinary woman... she wants to draw him [Paul] out and absorb him till there is nothing left of him, even for himself. He will never be a man on his own feet – she will suck him up" (Lawrence 1992: 230). From the start, she sees Miriam as a major opponent, one who can compete on equal footing with her. From Miriam's depiction, parallels between these two women can be drawn. First, "romantic in her soul", Miriam is said to have "something of a princess" (Lawrence 1992: 173), a reference which echoes Gertrude's portrayal at the beginning of the novel, when she is said to have still "preserved his [John Field's] Bible and kept his memory intact in her heart" (Lawrence 1992: 16). Then, the emphasis on Miriam's "trembling and passionate love for Christ and God" (Lawrence 1992: 173) reveals her fervent religious faith, which parallels Mrs. Morel's puritan upbringing. Also, like Mrs. Morel, Miriam is convinced that education is the key to upward mobility. She believes that "the world would have a different face for her and a deepened respect" (Lawrence 1992: 174) if she becomes well-read. Miriam speaks a feminist language, for instance when she overtly complains about women's social condition and expresses her desire to see changes. She declares: "I want to do something. I want a chance like anyone else. Why should I, because I'm a girl, be kept at home and not allowed to be anything? What chance have I?" (Lawrence 1992: 185). The use of the rhetorical questions demonstrates how passionate she is about equal rights for women. However, Brian Finney remarks, in Miriam's discourse "the entire enterprise of education becomes confused with a sense of class snobbery" (Finney 1990: 41). Miriam feels like "she was different from other folk, and must not be scooped up among the common fry. Learning was the only distinction to which she thought to aspire" (Lawrence 1992: 174). Here, Miriam's statement parallels and reminds the reader of Mrs. Morel's patronizing attitude when she first moved to the Bottoms. As the daughter of a big family, Miriam also assumes the role of mother figure to her youngest brother, who she holds "in her arms, she swayed slightly from side to side with love" (Lawrence 1992: 184). Then forcing the child to show affection for her, she insists by constantly asking him "you love me, don't you?" (ibd.). Her continual need to be loved and reassured is the first evidence of her narcissistic need. If at first, Miriam's maternal behaviour acts in her favour when it comes to winning Paul's affection, for the latter is continuously craving motherly nurturance and tries to replicate the connection that ties him to his mother through his relationship with Miriam, and again with Clara, as their relationship progresses, Paul experiences the constraint that this affair represents for him. Later, he eventually confirms his mother's observation when he reproaches the young lady for her destructive tendency. He asked her "Can you never like things without clutching them as if you wanted to pull the heart out of them?" (Lawrence 1992: 257) and blames her for "always begging things to love you [...] even the flowers, you have to fawn on them" (Lawrence 1992: 258). He harshly tells her "You don't want to love – your eternal and abnormal craving is to be loved. You aren't positive, you're negative. You absorb, absorb, as if you must fill yourself up with love, because you've got a shortage somewhere" (ibd.). The image of the squashed flowers is a direct analogy to Paul's feeling of entrapment, as he experiences the weight of Miriam's control over him, as well as her overwhelming tendency to dominate and possess others. Paul's crude words are reminiscent of his mother's belief that Miriam seeks to absorb her son, which emphasizes her ability to read into others, at the same time as it reveals Miriam's narcissistic features. As Paul points out, Miriam "has to fill herself up with love, because she has got a shortage somewhere" (Lawrence 1992: 258). Perhaps, the "shortage" in question is the illustration of Miriam's narcissistic wound, stemming from her subjugation to the oppressive rule of her brothers, who constantly ridicule and mistreat her. Expressed in free indirect style, Paul's opinion of his girlfriend is provided. He believes that "her soul was naked in her great dark eyes, and there was the same yearning appeal upon her" (Lawrence 1992: 226). Violeta Sotirova questions Paul's statement: "Miriam is described as having the *same* yearning appeal. *Same* as what?" (Sotirova 2011: 142). She notes that "Although formally linked to the preceding sentence with a conjunction, it is semantically impossible to attribute it to Paul because it contradicts his interpretation of Miriam's state" (ibd.). The words "yearning" and "yearned" parallel the repetition of the word "wait" in connection with Mrs. Morel who is constantly depicted as waiting on Paul, for instance in "Mrs. Morel clung now to Paul [...] *She waited* for him to come home in the evening" (*my emphasis*; Lawrence 1992: 142), or again "it was as if the pivot and pole of his life, from which he could not escape, was his mother. / And in the same way *she waited for him*. In him was established her life now" (*my emphasis*; Lawrence 1992: 261). The repetition of the words "wait" and "yearn" reveals Paul's acknowledgment that both Miriam and his mother strongly desire him and seek to possess him. Finally, whether Gertrude's hostility for Miriam is a consequence of her possessive love for Paul or stems from clarity of thoughts, her assessment of Miriam is proven to be accurate.

Therefore, when Paul finally breaks up with Miriam, he saves himself from another consuming and confining relationship.

3.4 EXONERATING THE MOTHER

Aware of Miriam's narcissistic features, the reader is led to question Mrs. Morel's share of responsibility for her son's break-up with her. Mrs. Morel is the first one to notice that Miriam is "pull[ing] the heart out" (Lawrence 1992: 257) of Paul. Nonetheless, as the novel progresses, it is revealed that it is Miriam's absorption rather than Gertrude's demands, which triggers Paul's emotional conflict. Accessing Paul's consciousness through free indirect speech, the narration points out that: "he [Paul] wanted now to give her passion and tenderness, and he could not. He felt that she wanted the soul out of his body, and not him" and that "she wanted to draw all of him into her" (Lawrence 1992: 231-232). Indeed, Paul is aware of the stakes that this relationship with Miriam represents for him. His impression echoes Gertrude's observation that Paul "could not go on with his work. He could do nothing. It was as if something were drawing his soul out towards Willey Farm. Then he put on his hat and went, saying nothing. And his mother knew he was gone" (Lawrence 1992: 231). In these two quotations, Sotirova notices the repetition of the phrases "*the soul out* of his body", "*to draw* all of him into her" (*my emphasis*; first quotation) and "*drawing his soul* out towards Willey Farm" (*my emphasis*; second quotation), which insists on the complicity existing between mother and son, showing that "Paul experiences Miriam's effect on him in much the same way as his mother, even though she [Mrs. Morel] had never communicated it to him verbally" (Sotirova 2011: 141). In this case, the use of repetition stresses the strong attachment between mother and son, which "is so profound that their consciousnesses fuse" (ibd.). While first, Miriam's possessive nature is introduced as one of the main causes of their break-up, later Paul's frustration is more and more expressed in sexual terms as in "now this 'purity' prevented even their first love-kiss. It was as if she could scarcely stand the shock of physical love, even passionate kiss, and then he was too shrinking and sensitive to give it [...]. And Paul hated her because somehow, she spoilt his ease and naturalness" (Lawrence 1992: 216). The previous quotation underlines Miriam's idealization of love as something spiritual instead of physical and shows her inability to fulfil Paul's sexual longing and need for intimacy. Paul reproaches her for her reluctance to yield to sensual love and compares their relationship to one between "a mystic monk to a mystic nun" (Lawrence 1992: 292). Reflecting upon their relationship, he writes to her "in all our relations no body enters. I do not talk to you through the senses – rather through the spirit. That is why we cannot love in the common sense..." (ibd.). He believes that "if people marry, they must live together as affectionate humans, who may be commonplace with each other without feeling awkward – not as two souls" (ibd.) and he clearly sees her physical aloofness as her inability to be "in touch with life" (Sagar 1989: 32). This marks a deep contrast with Clara's sensual spontaneity, which allows them to rapidly become intimate. When it comes to Paul's relationship with Clara, despite her warnings to her son "you'll tire of her, my son; you know you will" (Lawrence 1992: 374), Mrs. Morel does not actively urge Paul to split from Clara; instead, she approves of Paul's new girlfriend, convinced that "at any rate that feeling was wholesome" (Lawrence 1992: 300). She even has her over for Sunday tea (see Lawrence 1992: 367-368). Clara is made welcome by the family and the words "feeling of balance", "cool, clear atmosphere" and "harmony" (Lawrence 1992: 367), which describe the tea time afternoon at the Morel's, not only indicate that the young lady felt at ease but also that she was immediately integrated. This thought emphasized by her feeling "she completed the circle" (Lawrence 1992: 367). Meanwhile, the disclosure of Miriam's awareness that she "has never been accepted as Clara has been" (Lawrence 1992: 368) reasserts on the one hand, Clara's outgoing nature which strongly contrasts with Miriam's reserved personality, while on the other hand, it suggests that Gertrude's disapproval of Miriam stems primarily from her being all too well aware of the negative repercussions that Miriam's narcissism might have on Paul. In that case, Mrs. Morel's reaction is one of a benevolent mother who has to show prudent vigilance over her son. When at the end of the novel, Paul decides to break up with Clara, it seems that for her son's decision, Mrs. Morel is not to be held accountable, at least not directly. While earlier Paul reproaches Miriam her lack of sensuality which, he believes, hinders their relationship from growing to maturity, the deterioration of his feelings for Clara is based on her inability to spiritually connect with him. Gămini Salgădo confirms that as the narrative progresses the reader "can feel the absence of feeling which marked Paul's relationship with Miriam and he feels it himself" (Salgădo 1996: 39). The following description: "he talked to her now with some of the old fervor with which he had talked to Miriam but he cared less about the talk; he did not bother about his conclusion" (Lawrence 1992: 317) shows that Paul's potential loss of interest in Clara is the result of her lack of abstraction of thoughts, which is intensified later on by him feeling trapped by the young woman's constant need for physical signs of affection:

> And she was mad with desire of him. She could not see him without touching him. In the factory, as he talked to her about spiral hose, she ran her hand secretly along his side. She followed him out into the basement for a quick kiss; her eyes, always mute and *yearning*, full of unrestrained passion, she kept fixed on his. He was afraid of her, lest she should too flagrantly give herself away before the other girls. She invariably *waited for him* at dinnertime for him to embrace her before she went. He felt as if she were helpless, almost a burden to him, and it irritated him.
> 'But what do you always want to be kissing and embracing for?' he said. 'Surely there's a time for everything'. (*my emphasis*; Lawrence 1992: 399)

This section, reported in free indirect discourse, offers a description of Clara, as seen and experienced through Paul. The use of the verbs "yearning" and "waited", is a *déjà vu* in the narration of Paul's feeling of entrapment in his relationship with women (Miriam and Gertrude). Through words such as "mad", "followed him", "unrestrained passion", Clara's excessive love for Paul is underlined, turning her into some kind of stalker and pitching Paul as her victim, and we are told that "he was afraid of her". Since this passage is largely told through Paul's point of view, it leads to an exaggerated and perhaps distorted representation of this woman's passion for him. It is also worth mentioning that Paul's viewpoint becomes increasingly unreliable in the later stages of the novel. This scene is also extremely suggestive of Paul's narcissistic personality. It is indicative of his sense of grandiosity or unrealistic sense of superiority which leads him to view his partners with disdain, while it excessively intensifies his impression of being loved. This idea is later confirmed when Clara refuses to divorce Baxter or when Miriam refuses his marriage proposal, thereby showing that Paul misrepresents the extent of these women's affection for him. Paul's narcissistic tendency is revealed first through his attachment to his mother. It is undeniable that Gertrude has a share of responsibility in promoting and sustaining an exclusive relationship with Paul. However, as the reader is told on several occasions, Gertrude did not want this child and only turned to him after the death of William. A close look at the novel shows that Paul, to some extent, encouraged his mother's strong attachment. As a child, Paul suffered from fits of depression, and these fits, although they did not often happen "caused a shadow in Mrs Morel's heart, and her treatment of Paul was different from that of the other children" (Lawrence 1992: 65). Gertrude's special treatment for Paul is justified by his fragile health condition, as the following statement makes obvious: "Paul was a rather delicate boy, subject to bronchitis. The others were all quite strong; so this was another reason for his mother's difference in feeling for him" (Lawrence 1992: 90). The boy's craving for exclusive maternal care is revealed in the child's feeling that the father "disturbed the atmosphere" (Lawrence 1992: 91) and in his refusal to allow Walter to look after him. Here, it is Paul who prevents his father from coming any closer to him, and not his mother. Also, enough examples in the novel show that Gertrude was pleased "when the children included the father in her heart" (Lawrence 1992: 64). She is "even glad that this child [Arthur] loved the father" (ibd.). Therefore, if the father appears to be "an outsider" (Lawrence 1992: 88) in the family, for this Gertrude cannot entirely be blamed. Walter's estrangement is not intentional but happened because he does not share the bourgeois values that his wife advocates and instils in the children. Mrs. Morel "gives always more than she receives" (Sagar 1989: 23) and her entire dedication to her son's happiness is even pathetic as a certain coldness takes place between mother and son, and Paul starts concealing things from her. Still, "discarded, she waited on him, cooked for him [...] and loved to slave for him" (Lawrence 1992: 324). This illustration of the maturation of the mother-son relationship again draws the attention on Paul's self-centeredness. He proves to be chiefly concerned with his own interests. As the narrative progresses, Paul's treatment of the women, who surround him, becomes highly manipulative and one-sided. In his relationships with women, he seeks to enhance his narcissistic pride. First, as a child and later on as a young adult, Paul is always on the lookout for compliments on and validations of his achievements from his mother, for example, after he won first-prize awards for two of his paintings, he is aware that his mother "felt a proud woman" (Lawrence 1992: 222). Nonetheless, Paul cannot be contented with minimal acknowledgement, therefore he tries to fish for compliments by asking her: "why don't you praise me up to the skies?" (Lawrence 1992: 221). Paul also seeks admiration from Miriam. The reader is told that "if he brought up his sketch-book, it was she who pondered longest over the last picture. Then she would look up at him" and would ask him: "Why do I like this so?" (Lawrence 1992: 182). This question would trigger some strong emotions in Paul: "always something in his breast shrank from these close, intimate, dazzled looks of hers" (ibd.). Paul's narcissistic pride is conveyed through Miriam's admiring look both at the paintings and the painter himself, reflected in the use of "look up" which indicates Paul's superiority, as well as Miriam's fascination for him.

Miriam sustains Paul's constant need for recognition and sparks the artist's inspiration, as the following statement suggests: "all his passion, all his wild blood, went into this intercourse with her, when he talked and conceived his work. She brought forth to him his imaginations" (Lawrence 1992: 241). Jack Stewart indicates that both "Paul's mother and Miriam stimulate his development in complementary ways" (Stewart 2005: 173). This thought which is best summed up in the following quotation: "in contact with Miriam he gained insight; his vision went deeper. From his mother he drew the life-warmth, the strength to produce" (Lawrence 1992: 190). In fact, Paul turns out to be mainly attracted to women who can serve his narcissistic self. First, he primarily seeks out Miriam's company when he needs her, as she herself comes to realize: "he seems to have come to her because he needed her so badly, and she listened to him, gave him all her love and her faith" (Lawrence 1992: 290). But Paul is unable to return the favour, as he himself tells his mother: "I even love Clara and I did Miriam; but to give myself to them in marriage I couldn't. I couldn't belong to them. They seem to want me and I can't ever give it them" (Lawrence 1992: 395). These examples make clear that Paul's self-centeredness is linked to his inability to commit himself to these women, from whom he draws either his inspiration or receives narcissistic satisfaction. He is depicted as enjoying the competition of these women over him, because it makes him feel important. He even encourages their rivalry, for instance by making Clara believe that the other female colleagues are envious of her because she has his special attention (see Lawrence 1992: 315-316). A similar situation occurs between Miriam and Gertrude. In this particular scene, despite his awareness of these women's hostility to each other, he perversely thinks "it was wonderfully sweet and soothing to sit there for an hour and a half next to Miriam, and near to his mother, uniting his two loves under the spell of the place of worship" (Lawrence 1992: 230). Again, this is one of the many instances, which points out Paul's inability to empathize with others.

In fact, Paul is mainly attracted to women who in his eyes could constitute "his steppingstones up into the middle class" (Finney 1990: 41) or contribute to his new experience of life, either sexually or spiritually. Then once they are of no more use to him, Paul "kills or discards" (ibd.) them. In his relationship with Clara, his manipulative nature is revealed, when he shamelessly gets rid of her after she is of no more use to him. Clara confirms that "he was a mean fellow, after all, to take what he wanted and then give her back. She did not remember that she herself had had what she wanted, and really, at the bottom of her heart, wished to be given back" (Lawrence 1992: 451). Paul's exploitative nature is underlined, and it is even worsened by the impression that at the end, he is the only one who got what he wanted, again referring to his narcissism. As for his relationship with Miriam, a similar pattern can be noticed. As mentioned before, whenever Miriam contributes to Paul's artistic advancement, she has his undivided attention and a special place in his life. However, when he notices that she cannot fulfil his sexual desires, he moves away from her on the basis that "there was something else he wanted. He could not be satisfied" (Lawrence 1992: 268). Even if he is aware that "he had landed her in a nasty hole, and was leaving her in the lurch" (Lawrence 1992: 340), he cannot accept being held accountable for it. Therefore, he displaces responsibility onto Miriam and thinks: "she had really played with him, not he with her. She had hidden all her condemnation from him, had flattered him, and despised him" (Lawrence 1992: 341). Paul's inability to take the blame for his actions further speaks for his narcissistic ego. When it comes to his relationship with his mother, critics have usually considered Mrs. Morel as an obstacle to Paul's well-being, and as the puppeteer who pulls the strings behind him. Jessie Chambers was convinced that "his mother conquered indeed, but the vanquished one was her son" and that "in *Sons and Lovers*, Lawrence handed his mother the laurels of victory" (Daleski 1988: 37), an impression which parallels Paul's assertion that "he could not be free to go forward with his own life, really love another woman" (Lawrence 1992: 389). If here Paul seems to realize the constraint his mother represents, his realization only occurs from the moment he notices his mother's physical weakening and understands that sooner or later, she will not be there for him any longer. When he realizes that his mother is ageing, Paul's first thoughts are again above all directed towards his own self. In the scene where mother and son undertake a walk to the cathedral, Paul notices his mother's difficulty to climb the hill. Infuriated by her physical weakness, he selfishly exclaims: "'What are you old for!' he said, mad with his impotence. 'Why can't you walk? Why can't you come with me to places?' [...] 'What's the good of that to *me*?' he cried, hitting his fist on the wall" (Lawrence 1992: 281-282). It is important to note the italicized "me", which stresses Paul's instinctive concern for himself, rather than for his mother's health. Then, his reaction of 'wanting to cry' and 'smash things in fury' is a result of his narcissistic rage, showing that he cannot accept to lose his mother's exclusive attention and admiration, which so far contributed to reinforcing his sense of pride. He also attempts to maintain his mother's dependence on him, because it provides him with the feeling of importance that he constantly longs for, which is why he insists on many occasions that "I'll never marry while I've got you – I won't" (Lawrence 1992: 286). In sustaining his mother's narcissistic needs and excessive love for him, he repeatedly swears allegiance to her, promising he will always remain by her side till her death, but at the same time he also fans false hopes with his empty promises. Paul describes their future together: "and then you s'll have a pony-carriage. See yourself – a little Queen Victoria trotting around" (ibd.). The fantastic world he tries to create only further contributes to alienating both mother and son. His idea of a "pretty little house", with a "pony-carriage...trotting around" belongs to a quirky fairy-tale world which he perversely creates. But Mrs. Morel, feeling that the end is near, shows her concerns for her son and expresses her motherly benevolence: "I shouldn't like to think of you going through your life without anybody to care for you and do – no" (Lawrence 1992: 285). Therefore, although Gertrude is a narcissistic mother, she also proves, on many occasions, to have her son's interests at heart. Thus, she cannot entirely be blamed for her son's inability to commit to other women, which has more to do with his thwarted emotional self and his self-centeredness rather than Gertrude's strong affection for him.

As Gertrude's health declines, so does Paul's attachment to his mother. Finally, in the chapter *The Release*, which focuses on Mrs. Morel's death and describes her long, painful suffering caused by cancer, the role between mother and child seems to be reversed. Paul is the one who looks after his mother on her death bed. First, calling her name such as "my pigeon", "my little" or "my love" (Lawrence 1992: 434), he seems to demonstrate affection for the sick child that his mother came to embody, which on the one hand reiterates the complicity existing between mother and son but on the other hand also reveals Paul's domination over her. Yet, when he decides to euthanize Gertrude, his decision first can be interpreted as an act of charity, for unable to witness his mother's suffering, he decides to relieve her from her pain and starts diluting her milk, before administrating an overdose of morphia. However, his generous act is to be questioned, for by so doing he contributes to weakening her, preventing any possible attempt at recovery and at the same time worsening her health condition. The image of Mrs. Morel being fed with milk reiterates the idea of her regression from adulthood to childhood. Milk which symbolizes fertility and life turns out to have a different meaning in this case. Ironically, Paul brings the milk in a "feeding-cup" (ibd.), and assures his mother that he tried it himself. But the perversion goes even further when Paul goes back to the kitchen to fetch some "clean milk" (ibd.). The choice of the adjective contributes to the reader's feeling of uneasiness, for from the start we are aware of its hidden meaning and become part of the plot. Instead of being an instrument of life, milk turns out to bring death and expresses the complete rejection of the maternal figure, by turning one of the most precious gifts of motherhood into a mortal poison.

The scene of the matricide (see Lawrence 1992: 437) is particularly ambiguous. While Paul's poisoning his mother can possibly be considered as mercy-killing, it can also be seen as an impulsive act. The arrangement of the sentences "suddenly her [Gertrude's] small voice wailed" to "another fibre seemed to snap in his [Paul's] heart" (Lawrence 1992: 437) conveys a strategic doubt, leading the reader to question the real cause of the sudden "snap in Paul's heart". Does this immediate reaction stem from Paul's irritation when facing his mother's commanding tone or did Paul read into the "dark bubbles" (ibd.) a pleading wish to be relieved from the pain once and for all? Perhaps he has realized that alive she is of no more use to him and since he is only able to take and not to give, he considers his mother a burden to him. An alternative interpretation of Paul's change of heart can be read alongside Karl Menninger's examination of a son's mother-fixation. He propounds that a son who is excessively attached to his mother might feel more hatred and fear than love toward her but will most likely "attempt to conceal his hostility to her" (Menninger 1942: 57). Possibly, this is what Paul did throughout his life till the very moment his mother's physical condition weakens, and she becomes more vulnerable and less to be feared. But if this matricide can be interpreted as a relief from the pain engendered by illness for the patient as well as the other members of the family, the reaction of these children delighted and rejoicing at the very thought of the mischief they are about to commit, frankly reveals their equivocal motives, which is worsened by the absence of guilt indicated by Paul's ability to sleep "almost immediately" (Lawrence 1992: 439) and later by him wondering if it would not be of any help "if he piled the blanket and heavy coats on her" (Lawrence 1992: 441). It is difficult to ignore Paul's cold-blooded thinking and the absence of guilt or regret after the deed.

Finally, Paul's description as "stepp[ing] softly backwards and forwards at his paintings" (Lawrence 1992: 437) can be interpreted as a metaphorical indication that his artistic inspiration has reached a stagnating stage linked to his mother's health condition. The narrative seems to suggest that this obstacle in his artistic production can only be overcome through the mother's death, which turns out to help in reviving the artist's imagination through his suffering, hence acting to some extent as a stimulant for Paul's sense of creativity. Richard Beards confirms: "whatever wounds the death of his mother aggravates in Paul, he imagines her star-like and ever-present...an encouragement to go on" (Beards 1974: 213), hence reiterating Mrs. Morel's further contributions to her son's accomplishment even beyond her lifetime. At the end of the novel, the picture of Paul "turning sharply" and "walk[ing] towards the city's gold phosphorescence" (Lawrence 1992: 464) indicates his ability to eventually grow out of his temporary depression and withdrawal that his mother's death has occasioned. At the same time, it refers to the protagonist's walk towards freedom and self-realization, suggested through the reference to the city, which Beards explains "has been the place where the ambitious have sought their challenge, have striven to define themselves" (Beards 1974: 215). Indeed, Paul's fate is reminiscent of Stephen Dedalus' in James Joyce's *A Portrait of an Artist as a Young Man* (1916), which similarly concludes with the artist's decision to leave his family and friends behind to become an artist. It seems that both Lawrence and Joyce underline the necessity for their protagonist to walk away from his community and to reject all socially imposed bonds in order to grow both personally and artistically. Both Paul and Stephen free themselves from family commitment in order to embrace the life of the artist, who is *per se* seen as an isolated figure. Paul has struggled throughout the novel to develop his artistic consciousness and it is finally, Fiona Becket comments, "in the closing lines of the book, [that] he achieves a sense of individual self-hood, free at last from the women in his life (mother, lovers) who have, up to that point, defined him" (Becket 2002: 44). Lastly, the novel's open ending suggests the existence of opportunities for the hero and thereby, concludes on a positive note. Accordingly, instead of ruining Paul's life, as many critics have argued, Mrs. Morel turns out to further encourage her son's talents as a painter, helping him to develop his artistic self, even after her death, hence leaving her imprint long after.

All in all, although Gertrude Morel qualifies as narcissistic mother, since she displays great need to be loved and admired, and at times also engages in exploitative relationships with William and Paul, she nonetheless cannot be completely condemned for attempting to assuage her own narcissistic needs through her sons. Lawrence reveals the other side of the coin through his minute depiction of an affectionate mother, who nurses her children until their last breath. Therefore, one cannot fully blame or entirely praise this mother for the excessive love she shows to her children. Keith Sagar declares that "the mother is presented as neither absolutely right nor absolutely wrong" (Sagar 1989: 24). Even if she may be found guilty of seeking reparative measures to make up for her narcissistic injury through her suffocating relationship with her sons, she still proves to worry about her children, envisioning for them a promising future, and on several occasions, warning them against possible dangers which could lead to their destruction. Consequently, the portrayal of Gertrude Morel challenges the hegemonic social norms which tend to see mothers as selfless, protective caretakers and negatively judge those who fail to meet these expectations. The novel also suggests that the socio-economic component needs to be considered in the re-evaluation of the narcissistic mother that Gertrude Morel embodies. D.H. Lawrence is not the only one who recognizes the influence of the socio-economic conditions of the time in encouraging and sustaining mothers' narcissistic injury, so does James Joyce in *Dubliners*, his collection of short stories.

4 Mothers and Social Criticism in James Joyce's *Dubliners*

James Joyce's negative representation of female characters has led many critics such as Sandra Gilbert and Susan Gubar to consider women in his fiction as "confined to her [their] body, excluded from the production of culture" (K. Lawrence 1990: 237). Others, such as Richard Ellmann have claimed that Joyce consistently depicted women as either virgin or whore. Suzette Henke sustains that "Joyce never transcended the catholic urge to stereotype women as untouched virgins or defiled prostitutes" (Henke 1980: 14). Indeed, women are often represented as unfaithful, too domineering or on the contrary completely powerless. However, in *Dubliners*, Joyce offers a more complex depiction of his female characters than the virgin/whore dichotomy. In his short stories, especially in "A Mother", "A Boarding House" and "A Painful Case", he depicts women who try to escape the narrow confines of the social and economic environment of the time by challenging the role they were ascribed. Kirsten Vera Van Rhee mentions that in the mid-nineteenth century, women were required to fulfil the traditional female roles of "self-sacrificing wives and mothers, submissive and humble to their husbands" (Van Rhee 2011: 5). She explains that young women were expected to "be virginal, emulating the Virgin Mary and families were to model themselves on the Holy Family" (ibd.), as advocated by the Irish Catholic Church. This shows that at that time the role of women in society was strongly constrained by their function as wife and mother. This question has tremendously influenced Joyce's novels, for example, in *Ulysses*, Leopold Bloom realizes that "home always breaks up when the mother goes" (Joyce 1998: 145) and he insists that mother's duty to her children is "to protect him as long as possible" (Joyce 1998: 106). These words indicate that Joyce does not underestimate the importance of mothers and maternal care in his writing, but quite the opposite. He places mothers as central figures in the three short stories examined in this chapter, thereby showing that besides the treatment of the issue of poverty, drunkenness, child abuse, and hypocrisy of the church, he seems to demonstrate deep interest in the question of cynical exploitation performed by women, in particular mothers, who are revealed to show signs of narcissism. This chapter investigates how through his satirical tone and his ambiguous depiction of mothers in "The Boarding House", "A Mother" and "A Painful Case", Joyce presents female parents as narcissistic beings, who try at all costs to seek reparation for their narcissistic injury through their relationship with their children or by engaging into a love affair with a younger man, in the case of Mrs. Sinico in "A Painful Case". However, even if at first glance the attitude of these mothers appears dubious and reprehensible, Joyce, in a similar way as D.H. Lawrence, encourages his readers to engage into a socio-economic reading of the texts. Through his representation of strong mother figures, Joyce seems to give a voice to these devoted mothers whose demands and needs have been completely ignored in this rather male-dominated society. Simultaneously, their analysis sheds light on Joyce's social criticism. Suzanne Nalbantian observes that these mothers "emerge in another process of transposition" (Nalbantian 1994: 111). She sees these industrious mothers and wives as "national types", namely as embodiment of "the abused motherlands in atrophy" (Nalbantian 1994: 112). However, if this analogy between the mother and Ireland is more explicit in *A Portrait of the Artist as a Young Man*, in which the mother is pictured at the end packing the bag of her son, who is about to leave the motherland, or in *Ulysses* through the character of Molly Bloom, who Suzette Henke sees as standing for "the new Ireland" (Nalbantian 1994: 112), explicit and direct comparison between the mother figures in "A Mother", "A Boarding House" and "A Painful Case" and the homeland are absent. Finally, Joyce by providing a psychological depth to his mother figures reminds us that "Art is not an escape from life. It's just the very opposite. Art, on the contrary, is the central expression of life" (Cixous 1972: 31) and thereby, he offers a more sympathetic description of Mrs. Kearney, Mrs. Mooney and Mrs. Sinico.

4.1 MOTHERS IN "THE BOARDING HOUSE" AND "A MOTHER"

4.1.1 Mrs. Mooney and Mrs. Kearney

With the intention of painting a portrait of Irish society, Joyce chooses to provide a complex description of *Dubliners*' mothers, hence bringing the reader to reflect upon human nature, and finally leading him to the conclusion that human beings can be deceitful. At first glance, the reader gets a positive image of Mrs. Mooney from "The Boarding House" and Mrs. Kearney in "A Mother". Mrs. Mooney's authoritarian attitude, when she forces Mr. Doran to marry Polly, her pregnant daughter, to some extent arouses sympathy for this single parent who only behaves like a protective mother, seeking to defend and restore the tarnished honour of her pregnant daughter:

> He [Bob Doran] had simply taken advantage of Polly's youth and inexperience: that was evident. The question was: What reparation would he make? [...] There must be reparation made in such cases. It is very well for the man: he can go his ways as if nothing had happened, having had his moment of pleasure, but the girl has to bear the brunt. Some mothers would be content to patch up such an affair for a sum of money; she had known cases of it. But she would not do so. For her only one reparation could make up

for the loss of her daughter's honour: marriage. (Joyce 2000: 48-49)

The passage mentioned above is revealing in a number of ways. First, emphasizing the daughter's 'youth' and 'inexperience', it clearly presents Polly and at the same time, Mrs. Mooney as victims of Mr. Doran's loose morals and appetite for sexual adventures. Then, by comparing Mrs. Mooney's decision with others facing the same issue, the text only strengthens the idea that Mrs. Mooney has only her daughter's best interest at heart, for she advocates Polly's union to Mr. Doran rather than accepting money as "reparation", like "some mothers" would have favoured. When it comes to Mrs. Kearney from "A Mother", she also appears at first sight to be defending Kathleen's interests. She fights for Kathleen's payment, so as to make sure that her daughter is not being manipulated and exploited by unscrupulous men such as Mr. Holohan and Mr. Fitzpatrick, the organizers of the concert. Even if these women use unconventional methods to help their children, they are forgiven since their act is understood as being strictly motivated by their love and benevolence towards their offspring. The reader almost sympathizes with these mothers who are standing up for their daughter's career and future in a society regulated by patriarchal ideals. However, Linda Rohrer Paige points out that "though *Dubliners* mothers may seem, on the surface, supportive and loving, under the veneer of apparent benevolence lurks an ugly side of motherhood" (Paige 1995: 1). Therefore, when the veneer is scraped off, one finally discovers that Mrs. Mooney is a cynical manipulator, who has insisted on Polly staying home to entertain the male lodgers instead of working as a typist in a corn-factor's office: "as Polly was very lively the intention was to give her the run of the young men. Besides young men like to feel that there is a young woman not very far away" (Joyce 2000: 47). It is also worth mentioning that the name of 'Mrs. Mooney' is strangely very close to the word 'Money'. This correlation can be interpreted as a sign for Mrs. Mooney's desire to climb the social ladder, even if it entails using her daughter as an attractive bait. As for Mrs.

Kearney, she also turns out to be a selfish being, who is perverted by success and who does not hesitate to "take advantage of her daughter's name" (Joyce 2000: 107) in order to reach her goal. Furthermore, what at first is understood as the fight for Kathleen's rights seems to be contradicted by Mrs. Kearney's confession that she is "asking for *my own* rights" (*my emphasis*; Joyce 2000: 116). The *dénouement* in the final scene demonstrates that the method she uses to achieve her ends proves to be more of a handicap than of a help to her daughter's reputation and career. However, the daughter is not the only one to face humiliation in front of the public. In the manner of a mirror, Kathleen's humiliation is reflected onto her mother, who takes the whole situation personally, and thus, confuses her identity with her daughter's. The idea of mirror image and reflection is relevant to the issue of narcissism, which affects the mothers in *Dubliners*.

First, it is important to mention that Joyce's inspiration from Greek mythology is not only expressed and limited to the composition of *Ulysses*, but also to be found within the characters present in *Dubliners*, who bear common features with Ovid's Narcissus. The author of the short stories places his characters interestingly in an environment where mirror reflections are facilitated. This is a dominant motif which also extensively appears in Jean Rhys' *Good Morning, Midnight*. The characters are surrounded by an endless number of reflective objects. For instance, in "The Boarding House", Mrs. Mooney is said to be "surveying herself in the pier-glass" (Joyce 2000: 49), while Polly is depicted as drying her eyes, looking at herself in the looking glass, before refreshing her eyes with the cool water from the water-jug (Joyce 2000: 51). In "A Mother", the same details can be noticed: Mrs. Kearney and her daughter can hardly avoid meeting their own reflections since the dressing-room is equipped with a mirror, in which the reader learns that "the artistes [...] glanced from time to time" (Joyce 2000: 108). Not only does Joyce surround his characters with reflective objects, but the importance of the gaze is also emphasized by the presence of a great amount of words and expressions related to eyesight. Furthermore, *Dubliners*' female characters turn out to display many features of individuals suffering from narcissism. For example, the ability to detect opportunities for self-enhancement is certainly presented in the person of Mrs. Mooney, who knows how and when to take advantage of the situation. Like a lion watching its prey, she watches the evolution of the affair between her daughter Polly and Mr. Doran from afar, waiting until the right time has come to act. Aware of Mr. Doran's social position and convinced that he has a well-paid job, she immediately recognizes the opportunity this love story represents for her daughter to have a comfortable future, as well as, and above all, the fulfilment of her own wish to climb the social ladder: "Besides, he had been employed for thirteen years in a great Catholic wine-merchant's office [...]. She knew he had a good screw for one thing and she suspected he had a bit of stuff put by" (Joyce 2000: 49). Warren Beck confirms in *Joyce's Dubliners: Substance, Vision, and Art*, "not that Mrs. Mooney is a mere schemer; she operates under a complete code and with vigilant responsibility according to her lights" (Beck 1969: 47). Beck also concludes that "she [Mrs. Mooney] is that rare remarkable parent who can combine unobtrusive permissiveness with precise concealed purpose" (Beck 1969: 151). Moreover, Mrs. Mooney can distinguish without any difficulties which customers "were only passing time away" from those who "mean business" (Joyce 2000: 47) with her daughter. Mrs. Mooney's cunning and manipulative character is best demonstrated by her ability to think logically and find arguments as well as counter-arguments, to force Mr. Doran into marrying Polly:

> She was sure she would win. To begin with she had all the weight of social opinion on her side: she was an outraged mother. She had allowed him to live beneath her roof assuming that he was a man of honour, and he had simply abused her hospitality. He was thirty-four or thirty-five years of age, so that youth could not be pleaded as his excuse; nor could ignorance be his excuse since he was a man who had seen something of the world. He had simply

taken advantage of Polly's youth and inexperience: that was evident. (Joyce 2000: 48)

Here, Mrs. Mooney's rhetorical skills are clearly exposed. Using the adverbial clause "to begin with", Mrs. Mooney introduces her first argument, also suggesting that there are many more to follow. Not only does she prepare and provide her case, but she also anticipates Bob Doran's possible counter-arguments in order to better debunk them. Obviously, her strategy consists in presenting her daughter and herself as victims of Doran's debauchery. At the same time, she plays on the social pressure and repercussions that such an affair might entail for his career: "[S]he did not think he would face publicity" or again "publicity would mean for him, perhaps, the loss of his sit" (Joyce 2000: 49).

As far as Mrs. Kearney is concerned, she turns out to be very ambitious as well. Her narcissistic behaviour is revealed by her desire to be promoted at her daughter's expense; she does not hesitate to use Kathleen's musical talent to enhance her own reputation. She makes her daughter appear marketable and, as mentioned earlier, wishes to "take advantage of her daughter's name" (Joyce 2000: 107). Like Mrs. Mooney, who carefully plans the affair between her daughter and Mr. Doran, she plans every detail of the concert:

> Mr Holohan, assistant secretary of the Eire Abu Society, had been walking up and down Dublin for nearly a month, with his hands and pockets full of dirty pieces of paper, arranging about the series of concerts. He had a game leg and for this his friends called him Hoppy Holohan. He walked up and down constantly, stood by the hour at street corners arguing the point and made notes; but in the end it was Mrs. Kearney who arranged everything. (Joyce 2000: 106)

The description of Mr. Holohan, which shows him "walking up and down", certainly points at his inability to make decisions, always going back to the same point. This statement is further justified by the content of his pockets, which were "full of dirty pieces of paper". The previous detail suggests his lack of organization and his difficulties in assembling different pieces together, thereby questioning his success in putting up a concert. Also, the closing statement of the passage ("but in the end it was Mrs. Kearney who arranged everything") marks a deep contrast to Holohan's lack of seriousness and again implies Mrs. Kearney's significant involvement in planning the project. Because she invests her time and energy in putting together the concert, she expects acknowledgment of her hard work from Mr. Holohan and the Eire Abu Society, her family and friends, as well as from the public. Recognizing in the concert a chance for self-enhancement, she strains to make it as perfect as possible:

> Mrs. Kearney brought some lovely blush-pink charmeuse in Brown Thomas's to let into the front of Kathleen's dress. It cost a pretty penny; but there are occasions when a little expense is justifiable. She took a dozen of two-shilling tickets for the final concert and sent them to those friends who could not be trusted to come otherwise. She forgot nothing and, thanks to her, everything that was to be done was done. (Joyce 2000: 108)

Again, the above quotation insists on Mrs. Kearney's contribution to the show and reveals how proud she feels about her achievement. In order to ensure that her accomplishment is acknowledged by those who know her, she even sends them tickets for the final concert. As a result, both Mrs. Mooney and Mrs. Kearney appear to be able to detect opportunities for self-enhancement, even if they have to take advantage of their daughters.

In addition, narcissists' tendency to devalue their relationship partners is not only noticeable through the character of Gertrude Morel in *Sons and Lovers* but is also disclosed through Mrs. Mooney and Mrs. Kearney's attitude towards their husband. In "The Boarding House", the devaluation of Mr. Mooney is illustrated by the negative description at the beginning of the story:

But as soon as his father-in-law was dead Mr Mooney began to go
to the devil. He drank, plundered the till, ran headlong into debt.
It was no use making him take the pledge: he was sure to break
out again a few days after. By fighting his wife in the presence of
customers and by buying bad meat he ruined his business. One
night he went for his wife with a cleaver and she had to sleep in a
neighbour's house. (Joyce 2000: 46)

This passage is reminiscent of the fight between Mr. and Mrs. Morel, ending up in Gertrude at the time pregnant with Paul, being locked out of the house by her drunk husband. Here, Joyce's use of the third-person narration which is focalized through the character of Mrs. Mooney strategically reflects her point of view, allowing the reader to access her personal thoughts on her marriage. Clearly, she is blaming her husband for his failure to manage *his* business (*my emphasis*). The use of the possessive pronoun "his" instead of "her" undoubtedly suggests that she holds her husband solely responsible for ruining the business. Also, the previous passage is built on a comparison, which further stresses the gap between Mr. Mooney and his wife. On the one hand, Mr. Mooney is depicted as aggressive, alcoholic, and lazy, while his wife, on the other hand, is very active and hard-working. She has the merit of raising her children on her own, while at the same time she professionally and successfully runs the boarding house. Finally, the oppressor-oppressed relationship is reversed in favour of Mrs. Mooney, who can decide that "she would give him [Mr. Mooney] neither money nor food nor house-room" (Joyce 2000: 46). Mrs. Mooney is also described as being "a big imposing woman" (ibd.), suggesting her superiority over her husband as well as the male customers of the boarding house.

When it comes to the relationship between Mrs. and Mr. Kearney, it becomes evident that it is not very different from that between Mrs. Mooney and her husband, showing the same passive-active dynamics. Mrs. Kearney is the one who does business with Mr. Holohan and Mr. Fitzpatrick. Throughout the story, her husband hardly speaks a word;

the reader does not even have access to his thoughts. His position of inferiority is further emphasized by his weakness related to his health problem: "his cough troubled him" (Joyce 2000: 107). Additionally, Mr. Kearney's attempt to ignore the discussion between his wife and Mr. Holohan by continuing to "strike his beard" (Joyce 2000: 14) betrays his desire to escape an uncomfortable situation towards which he feels powerless. Finally, his status as a man is challenged by the way Mrs. Kearney thinks of his role in the family: "his wife appreciated his *abstract* value as a male" (*my emphasis*; Joyce 2000: 110). She also does not hesitate to order her husband in the same way as she would give directives to her servants, for example, when she commands him to get a cab at the end of the story (see Joyce 2000: 106). Lastly, it can be concluded that Mrs. Kearney is the one who serves as authority figure in the household. Furthermore, it is revealed that both Mrs. Kearney and Mrs. Mooney demonstrate emotional aloofness in their relationship with their husbands, while they tend to vigorously focus their attention on their daughters.

4.1.2 Daughters as Objects of Possession

In fact, Mrs. Mooney and Mrs. Kearney are best represented through their relationship with their daughters. Joyce seems to suggest that mothers are those who are most prone to narcissistic behaviour, for mothers tend to retain a powerful connection with their child and keep considering him/her as an extension of their own selves. Therefore, it is important to mention that both Mrs. Kearney and Mrs. Mooney share the same life experiences as their daughters, (which also applied to Virginia Woolf's mother figure Mrs. Ramsay in *To the Lighthouse*). When it comes to Polly, not only does she work in the boarding house with her mother, but her innocence in the whole affair is compromised. She is said to "look like a little perverse Madonna" (Joyce 2000: 47), thereby underlining her ambivalence. In an earlier manuscript of "The Boarding House", Joyce described Polly's eyes as giving her the look of a "little hypocritical Madonna" (Beck 1969: 147), a statement that is reiterated when she sings: "I'm a...naughty girl. / You needn't sham: / You know I am" (Joyce 2000: 47). Not only does Polly bear the features of a manipulator, she also appears to secretly connive with her mother:

> She had been made awkward by her not wishing to receive the news in too cavalier fashion or to seem to have connived and Polly had been made awkward not merely because allusions of that kind always made her awkward but also she did not wish it to be thought that in her wise innocence she had divined the intention behind her mother's tolerance. (Joyce 2000: 48)

Additionally, her eyes are also described as "looking upwards" (Joyce 2000: 47), confirming once again that she is a social climber, just like her mother is. Therefore, she finally appears not to be any better than her mother, but much more of the same kind. The narcissistic behaviour of mother figures becomes even more obvious when they start mistaking their identities for that of their daughters. Even if Mrs. Mooney was unlucky in her marital life, one can guess that she married her husband, hoping he would be good to her. Her traumatic experience as a spouse accounts for her desire to relive her life through Polly. By securing a respectable man for her daughter, she believes that she can realize her own dreams and do herself justice. This identity issue is also perceptible in the unspoken connivance that exists between mother and daughter: "in her [Polly's] wise innocence she had divined the intention behind her mother's tolerance" (Joyce 2000: 48). Finally, to quote Margot Norris, "Polly's restorative gestures, 'refreshing' her eyes and adjusting her hairpin in profile, appear to have all the calculation that would make her her mother's daughter" (Norris 1997: 164), demonstrating that both mother and daughter show the same manipulative behaviour and the same cynical thoughts.

When it comes to Mrs. Kearney, the confusion of her identity is best reflected by an inadvertent slip of the tongue, when she declares: "I'm asking for my own rights" (Joyce 2000: 116). Moreover, the repeated call for revenge underlines Mrs. Kearney's self-concern that overrides her consideration for her daughter. She seeks to valorise herself at the expense of Kathleen, and thus oppresses her child. Another important element relevant to the issue of narcissistic mothers is the name Mrs. Kearney chose for her daughter. According to Mary Power in "The Stories of Public Life":

> Mention of the name Kathleen Kearney conjures up the heroine of an old Irish song – "O, did you not hear of Kate Kearney? / She lives on the banks of Killarney," – and inadvertently perhaps, a popular Cockney music hall *artiste* of the day, Kate Carney. While many starlets invent stage names to suit their theatrical aspirations or metaphysical ideas of self, here the appropriate name may precede both mother's and daughter's ambitions. Kathleen Kearney is a name which predestines its bearer for a musical career, though the Kathleen of Joyce's story is never referred to casually as Kate. (Power 1997: 218-219)

The previous passage points out the early ambition of Mrs. Kearney, who already at her daughter's birth saw an opportunity to live out her dream of a musical career through her child, hence naming her after a famous singer.

Moreover, in both cases father figures are extremely discreet if not completely absent from the life of Kathleen and Polly, which, according to psychological assumptions, negatively impacts on the well-being of the daughters. The silence of the fathers in both short stories echoes their symbolical absences from the lives of their daughters, again preventing them from achieving psychic autonomy, leaving Polly and Kathleen no other choice but to live according to their mothers' desires. As a matter of fact, "narcissism condemned the mothers we encountered to profound psychic and emotional isolation" (Jensen 2011: 386), which is especially evident in the case of Mrs. Kearney, who ends up misunderstood and condemned by the artists and the committee, with nobody to side with her, not even her own family: "After that

Mrs. Kearney's conduct was condemned on all hands: everyone approved of what the Committee has done. She stood at the door, haggard with rage, arguing with her husband and daughter" (Joyce 2000: 116).

Consequently, oppressed by their mothers' self-absorption, both Polly and Kathleen are victimized. Polly's mother is known as "The Madam" by the young men who live in the boarding house. The name "Madam" is suggestive of her scrupulous managing of the house but also bears the connotation of someone in charge of a brothel, a procuress. Moreover, the text points out that "the boarding house was beginning to have a certain fame" (Joyce 2000: 50) and that Mrs. Mooney saw in Polly's vivacity a means to contribute to the family business: "As Polly was very lively the intention was to give her the run of the young men" (Joyce 2000: 47). Therefore, Mrs. Mooney is revealed to be prostituting her daughter to some degree. Mrs. Kearney also occupies a similar role. On many occasions in the story, Joyce engages in a word play over Mrs. Kearney's 'ladylike' behaviour: "'I thought you were a lady', said Mr. Holohan, walking away from her" or "'That's a nice lady!'" (Joyce 2000: 116). The emphasis on the word "lady" implies that Mrs. Kearney is "an outraged Madame [and], no 'lady'" (Paige 1995: 333). Also, Linda Rohrer Paige remarks, "Joyce carefully colors the concert scene with hues of sexual ambiguity" (ibd.). She further adds that the male characters' "clapping and stamping in the hall [...] punctuated by whistling" (Joyce 2000: 114) "seems better suited to a brothel than to a theater" (Paige 1995: 333). Yet, as Paige explains, "the playful progression of word choices here, 'clapping', 'stamping', 'whistling', 'panting', and 'burst[ing]', coupled with the men's 'content[ment]' following the 'scandalous exhibition', all point to Kathleen's success as a consummate entertainer" (Paige 1995: 334). Kathleen's experience on the stage is comparable to a sexual performance. Both Kathleen and Polly can be said to be passive characters, who suffer from the decisions made by their mothers. They never stand up for themselves and the reader never gets to read their thoughts. Every single gesture is perfectly controlled and directed by Mrs. Mooney and Mrs. Kearney, who mould the girls so as to turn them into mere polished surfaces that reflect their mother's images.

4.1.3 Exonerating Mrs. Mooney and Mrs. Kearney

However, even if Mrs. Mooney and Mrs. Kearney appear to be driven by their narcissistic needs, which at times results in the unfortunate victimization of their daughters, it is difficult to completely condemn these women for striving to improve their children's as well as their own social condition, especially when one considers the social and financial landscape of the time. Terence Brown precisely describes the economic decline of Dublin, which went from second largest city in the British Isles and among the ten largest cities in Europe at the time of the Union to merely fifth in the UK rankings by 1860, and finally, by the end of the century suffered the humiliation of being overtaken by Belfast as Ireland's largest city (see Brown 1992: xvii-xviii). Brown observes that "symptoms of stagnation and concomitant human misery were not hard to find" (Brown 1992: xviii). He explains that because of the absence of any productive industrial base, the majority of the Dubliners were employed in construction, in industries such as biscuit-making and brewing, in domestic service and in dock-work. But the decline in the docks led to severe unemployment, which added to the lower-middle-class' financial burden and increased poverty, mainly visible through the dwellings' conditions (see Brown 1992: xviii-xix). Brown reports that "many of the city's laboring and unemployed poor lived in the tenements for which the city was notorious" (Brown 1992: xix). These accommodations were "squalid, decaying Georgian townhouses" located "on streets and squares on the north side of the river in central Dublin which had once been the height of fashion, but by the early twentieth century were given over to slum conditions of the worst kind" (ibd.). They were often 'single rooms shared by three to six, or sometimes seven to twelve people' (ibd.). Since financial hardship threatened the majority of the inhabitants, one can easily understand why and how these mothers came to be so money-driven and opportunistic. Although only three stories in *Dubliners* offer a woman as central character, one cannot help noticing that women are those who suffer most in this exiguous social sphere, where job opportunities for young women were even more limited than for men. He explains that the teaching and nursing professions were mainly perpetuated by those in religious life, while married women would have access to the commercial world (as shopkeepers or landladies). Brown concludes that:

> in a country where marriages were often postponed to very advanced ages indeed, marital opportunities were few. So outside of domestic service, a post as a shop assistant, secretarial work, of the kind Polly Mooney undertakes for a time in 'The Boarding House', only Dublin's rich musical life offered real chance of a satisfying career. (Brown 1992: xxv)

Accordingly, aware of the socio-economic circumstances of the time, it is hard to blame Mrs. Kearney for her aggressive ambition and her opportunistic desire to launch Kathleen's musical career. Likewise, we can readily understand Mrs. Mooney's scheming to secure a husband for her daughter. Consequently, Joyce to some extent appears to exonerate these narcissistic mothers by stressing and demonstrating how their actions are finally determined and motivated by their anxiety about economic survival. In "The Boarding House" and "A Mother", Joyce stresses how society encourages and maintains mothers' narcissistic behaviour and underlines how narcissism becomes a means for self-preservation. This idea of narcissism as protection of one's self leads to the analysis of another narcissistic mother figure in *Dubliners*, through the portrayal of Mrs. Sinico in "A Painful Case".

4.2 MRS. SINICO'S EMOTIONAL EMPATHY

After writing "A Painful Case", Joyce thought it was one of his weakest stories, along with "After the Race". He was far from imagining that later, critics would consider it one of his most "profoundly psychological and emotionally resonant stories" (Beck 1969: 236). Many readings have been conducted on "A Painful Case", mostly focusing on the character of James Duffy and his possible repressed homosexuality. Departing from previous traditional interpretations of "A Painful Case", the focus on the character of Mrs. Sinico offers a fresh perspective on the question of 'self' in relation to narcissism. Even if she seems to play a secondary role in the story and is only introduced in relation to Duffy, her contribution to Joyce's social criticism cannot be ignored.

4.2.1 Establishing Mrs. Sinico as Narcissistic Mother

The story opens with a description of Mr. Duffy, a meticulous bank cashier who lives in a remote suburb of Dublin and has little social contact. Very organized and predictable, he generally eats at the same restaurant and occasionally attends a concert or an opera. It is at one of those concerts that one night James Duffy makes the acquaintance of Mrs. Emily Sinico, a married mother, who happened to be sitting next to him at the Rotunda. Their encounter is related as follows:

> He was surprised that she seemed so little awkward. While they talked he tried to fix her permanently in his memory. When he learned that the young girl beside her was her daughter he judged her to be a year or so younger than himself. Her face, which must have been handsome, had remained intelligent. It was an oval face with strongly marked features. The eyes were very dark and steady. Their gaze began with a defiant note but was confused by what seemed a deliberate swoon of the pupil into the iris, revealing for an instant a temperament of great sensibility. The pupil reasserted itself quickly, this half-disclosed nature fell again under the reign of prudence, and her astrakhan jacket, moulding a bosom of a certain fullness, struck the note of defiance more definitely. (Joyce 2000: 83-84)

In this passage, the narration focuses on Mrs. Sinico's physical as well as emotional description through Duffy's point of view. His attention appears to be drawn first to the lady's face, dwelling on her eyes, which reveal "a temperament of great sensibility" but also of boldness, before switching to her generous "bosom", which is interpreted by the young man as a clear sign of "defiance". This observation on Duffy's part shows that he is not indifferent to Mrs. Sinico's sensuality, at the same time as the emphasis on the lady's "defiance" (mentioned twice in this passage) indicates his awareness that Emily Sinico is an audacious woman who could potentially give in to her sexual urges. Words such as "moulding" and "fullness" chosen to describe the woman's bosom stress Mrs. Sinico's sexuality and offers a representation of this mother as a sexually attractive individual. Duffy appears to be fascinated by Mrs. Sinico and even if he meets both mother and daughter at the concert, he barely notices the daughter, and then, only "as a gauge to the mother's age" (Norris 2003: 161). However, the reference to the daughter, as brief as it is, turns out to be an essential element in establishing Mrs. Sinico as narcissistic mother. First, by pointing at the age gap existing between Duffy and Mrs. Sinico, Joyce introduces this mother's desire to remain young, at the same time as this information posits a possible rivalry between mother and daughter when it comes to winning Duffy's affection. This idea is further brought to light by Captain Sinico's interpretation of the young man's frequent visits as a sign of Duffy's interest in his daughter Mary. Therefore, he even encourages these visits, "thinking that his daughter's hand was in question" (Joyce 2000: 84). Mrs. Sinico's affair with the bank cashier appears to be a double betrayal, on the one hand of her husband and on the other hand of her daughter. Gradually, the portrait of narcissistic mother is unravelled, mainly when the reader learns that Captain Sinico "had dismissed his wife so sincerely from his gallery of pleasures that he did not suspect anyone else would take an interest in her" (Joyce 2000: 84). Obviously, Captain Sinico underestimates her seductiveness but also denies her sexual needs. In addition, his conviction that no other man could find her attractive denigrates his wife. Then, the reference to

Captain Sinico's "gallery of pleasures" seems to suggest that he might equally be conducting some extramarital relations. Mrs. Sinico tries to make up for her marital dissatisfaction and her lack of sexual fulfilment by engaging in a love affair with young Duffy, who to some extent soothes her needs.

Being denied the love and the attention she expects from her husband, Mrs. Sinico slowly yields to Duffy's sexual advances, which comfort her and prove to impact positively on her self-esteem, and by extension on her narcissistic self, which longs to be petted and flattered. Not only does James Duffy give Emily Sinico the impression of being desired and valued again but she slowly realizes that they might have more in common than one might think. Indeed, many critics have read James Duffy as "the epitome of Irish paralysis, a person so obsessed with his mental cohesion that he is incapable of any interaction with others" (DeVault 2010: 82). Duffy's less attractive features are brought to light, first through his "wish[ed] to live as far as possible from the city to which he was a citizen" (Joyce 2000: 82), which indicates as Christopher DeVault observes Duffy's rejection not simply of the city but also of the Dubliners. It further points at "his disinterest in interacting with anyone and his repulsion towards existences different from his own" (ibd.). This idea is confirmed by Joyce when he further depicts his protagonist as a man with "neither companions nor friends, church nor creed" (Joyce 2000: 83), a person whose "'[abhorrence]' of 'anything which betokened physical or mental disorder' prevents him from affirming otherness" (DeVault 2010: 82). Besides, Duffy's self-centeredness is also pointed out when Joyce notes that:

> He lived at a little distance from his body, regarding his own acts with doubtful side – glances. He had an odd autobiographical habit which led him to compose in his mind from time to time a short sentence about himself containing a subject in the third person and a predicate in the past tense. He never gave alms to beggars and walked firmly, carrying a stout hazel. (Joyce 2000: 83)

First, Duffy's exile encourages him to reflect solely on his own condition, then the allusion to his "autobiographical habit" of building "a short sentence about himself ... in the *third person*" (*my emphasis*) stresses his experiencing his body as an 'other self', like Narcissus did. Moreover, Duffy is revealed to be someone who thinks highly about himself and is staunchly convinced of his socio-political ideas. To Mrs. Sinico's suggestion to write out his thoughts, he answers scornfully: "For what, he asked her [...]. To compete with phrasemongers, incapable of thinking consecutively for sixty seconds? To submit himself to the criticisms of an obtuse middle class which entrusted its morality to policeman and its fine arts to impresarios?" (Joyce 2000: 85). Here, through the use of negatively loaded words, such as "phrasemongers", "incapable" or "obtuse", Duffy places himself as superior to the middle-class, which he judges too senseless and limited to understand his intellectual approach, hence suggesting that he is pretentious and full of himself. As established so far, both Mrs. Sinico and Duffy are revealed to be narcissistic characters, who find in this love affair a mirror to their self-image. Also, both Mr. Duffy and Mrs. Sinico are alienated by society. In Duffy's case, his alienation is expressed through the hermit-lifestyle he chooses to lead, while Mrs. Sinico's marginalization is conveyed through Joyce's depiction of the mother as "obliged to live utterly without interlocution or dialogic possibility" (DeVault 2010: 81). Finally, both characters find in each other a companion who could extract them from their loneliness and desolation.

4.2.2 Beneficial Aspects of the Illicit Love Affair

First, the love affair between Mrs. Sinico and Duffy is evocative of a relationship between mother and son. The following description sheds light on the nature of their relationship:

> Little by little he entangled his thoughts with hers. He lent her books, provided her with ideas, shared his intellectual life with her. She listened to all.

Sometimes in return for his theories she gave out some fact of her own life. With almost maternal solicitude she urged him to let his nature open to the full; she became his confessor. (Joyce 2000: 84)

Besides the age gap between Emily Sinico and James Duffy, pointed out earlier, the phrase "maternal solicitude" reinforces the idea that Mrs. Sinico shows motherly love and interest for Duffy and thus, that their attachment to one another is reminiscent of one between mother and son. Interestingly, Joyce uses words such as "entangled", "shared" and "urged" which not only mark a deep contrast from previous descriptions of these two as lonely and aloof individuals but indicate the emergence of a union and dependence between those two. At the same time, these words suggest a clinging type of affection, specific to narcissistic mothers. Indeed, the word "entangled" which refers to the action of twisting or wrapping together postulates the existence of a symbiotic relationship between Emily Sinico and James Duffy, a claim that is emphasized when Joyce writes:

He went often to her little cottage outside Dublin; often they spent their evenings alone. Little by little, as their thoughts entangled, they spoke of subjects less remote. Her companionship was like a warm soil about an exotic. Many times she allowed the dark to fall upon them, refraining from lighting the lamp. The dark discreet room, their isolation, the music that still vibrated in their ears united them. This union exalted him, wore away the rough edges of his character, emotionalized his mental life. Sometimes he caught himself listening to the sound of his own voice. (Joyce 2000: 85)

Here, Joyce deliberately misuses or plays with the word "alone". Since Mr. Duffy and Mrs. Sinico keep each other company in the evening, they are theoretically not really 'alone', in the sense of solitude and loneliness. However, by using the word 'alone', Joyce stresses the idea that these two are one (reinforced by the repetition of 'entangled' which already appeared in the previous quotation), showing that they are interdependent, and that this symbiosis is actually a relationship of mutual benefit and dependence. This bond between Mrs. Sinico and Duffy is to some extent reminiscent of the one between Gertrude Morel and Paul in *Sons and Lovers*, a relation driven by one's personal interests and characterized by possessiveness and exclusivity. Again, this is especially conveyed through the word "alone" and later on in Duffy's request to be invited to his lover's home, which indicates his desire to be officially part of her circle of relatives and acquaintances, rather than remaining external and hidden as his status as lover might seem to require. While Emily Sinico finds her sexual needs fulfilled and her narcissistic injury soothed, James Duffy experiences 'otherness' through his union with Mrs. Sinico. Also, positive changes arise from his relationship with this narcissistic mother, who through her compassion and maternal benevolence proves to bring the best out of her lover. This is best embodied through Joyce's observation that "the union *exalted* him, *wore away* the rough edges of his character, *emotionalized* his mental life" (*my emphasis;* Joyce 2000: 85). DeVault agrees on the mutually beneficial and positive influence that these two characters have on each other. He notes that "not only does she treat Duffy with kindness, but her encouragement to 'let his nature open to the full' constitutes a loving embrace that could counteract the personal and societal alienation of both characters" (DeVault 2010: 81). Furthermore, he interprets Mrs. Sinico's "maternal solicitude" (Joyce 2000: 84) as "an invitation for Duffy to develop more productive relations not just with her, but with his fellow Dubliners" (DeVault 2010: 81). Here, Joyce shows that a narcissistic mother can still demonstrate maternal benevolence and affection, and that all in all narcissism and empathy can co-exist within the same individual. However, when Duffy finally rejects Emily Sinico, he reveals his difficulty to overcome his internal conflict between self-love and love for others.

Duffy's internal crisis is best embodied when in a brief moment of clarity, he hears his own voice "insisting on the soul's incurable loneliness" and telling him that "we cannot give ourselves, it said: we are our own" (Joyce 2000: 85). And troubled by Mrs. Sinico's sign of affection, who is said to have "shown every sign of unusual excitement" and in a tremendous outpouring of fondness "caught up his hand passionately and pressed it to her cheek" (ibd.), Duffy decides to put an end to their relationship. His rash decision to break up with Mrs. Sinico, whose motherly care has proved beneficial to him, brings to attention his self-absorption which surely contrasts with Mrs. Sinico's narcissistic tendency. Throughout the story, Joyce appears to stress the positive aspects of Emily Sinico's narcissism. At the same time, he emphasizes the ravaging consequences of Duffy's self-interest. From the description of their encounter at the concert, Joyce indicates that a significant discrepancy exists between these two individuals' response to their surroundings. Even if Mrs. Sinico is portrayed as a narcissistic mother, her compassionate reaction to the concert's low attendance casts light on her ability to empathize with others. Joyce writes:

> The house, thinly peopled and silent, gave distressing prophecy of failure. The lady who sat next him looked round at the deserted house once or twice and then said:
> –What a pity there is such a poor house to–night! It's so hard on people who have to sing to empty benches. (Joyce 2000: 83)

Here, the disparity between their receptions of the concert is striking. While Mrs. Sinico instinctively feels sorry for the performers who "have to sing to empty benches", Mr. Duffy interprets the low attendance as a "distressing prophecy of failure". Mrs. Sinico's reaction, which points at her ability to empathize with others, marks a clear contrast to James Duffy's lamentation and disappointment in the concert, which reveals his tendency of bringing everything back to himself. The contradictory reactions to the same situation constitute the first comparison that exposes the essential differences in their narcissistic tendencies. Mrs. Sinico's ability to response empathetically is reminded at many occasions in the text, first through her "temperament of great sensibility" (Joyce 2000: 84) which diverges from Duffy's "saturnine" (Joyce 2000: 82) condition, then by her ability to be a listener to others. The reader learns that "he lent her books, provided her with ideas, shared his intellectual life with her. She listened to all [...] she became his confessor" (Joyce 2000: 84). This representation of Mrs. Sinico as a "confessor" accounts on the one hand for her motherly benevolence, and on the other hand, it provides further evidence of the discrepancy in their attitude towards others. Eventually, the alienating portrayal of James Duffy's narcissism serves Joyce's rhetorical purposes in establishing the narcissistic mother figure as "the living embodiment of empathy [...] a person whose alienation does not prevent her from aggressively loving and affirming the others she meets" (DeVault 2010: 97). However, even if Joyce allows a more positive reading of this mother, who is capable of demonstrating affection for others, the character of Mrs. Sinico nonetheless retains her narcissistic qualities till the end. Indeed, it is important to emphasize that her attraction to Duffy is and remains stimulated by her need to be loved. Such a situation, according to Freud contributes immensely to the reinforcement of an individual's self-esteem, while in a love relationship, not being loved results in lowering one's self-regard, which eventually happens when James Duffy breaks up with Mrs. Sinico, leading this traumatized mother to experience an extreme feeling of despair, which culminates in her tragic death at the end of the story.

4.2.3 Blaming the Lover, Exonerating the Mother

Joyce establishes a favourable portrayal of this narcissistic mother, who at the end can hardly be blamed for conducting an illicit romance with a younger man. First, by implying that Captain Sinico has lost interest in his wife and by suggesting that he might himself be having some affairs, Joyce clears Emily Sinico of any wrongdoing and the reader is invited to consider her extra-marital relationship with Duffy as a means for self-preservation and a way to seek narcissistic reparation. Furthermore, it is important to note that Duffy is the one who initiates their liaison. Joyce writes that "he met her again a few weeks afterwards at a concert in Earlsfort Terrace and seized the moments when her daughter's attention was diverted to become intimate" (Joyce 2000: 84). Noteworthy here is Joyce's use of free indirect discourse which gives access to Duffy's methodical way of thinking. Then, Joyce's choice of pronoun in the previous quotation is significant, for by privileging the use of the third person pronoun 'he' in "he met her again... and seized the moments" referring to James Duffy instead of 'they', he insists on Duffy's active implication in encouraging Mrs. Sinico's extra-marital relationship. At the same time, this description emphasizes his scheming intention and thereby further stresses Emily Sinico's passive involvement. Also, later on in the story the reader learns that:

> Meeting her a third time by accident he found courage to make an appointment. She came. This was the first of many meetings; they met always in the evening and chose the most quiet quarters for their walks together. Mr Duffy, however, had a distaste for underhand ways and, finding that they were compelled to meet stealthily, he forced her to ask him to her house. (Joyce 2000: 84)

Again, Duffy's implication in talking Mrs. Sinico into engaging in an extra-marital relationship cannot be ignored. Not only is he the one who initiates their meetings but he "forced her" to receive him at her house. Finally, when Duffy chooses to dismiss Emily Sinico on the account that "every bond...is a bond of sorrow" (Joyce 2000: 85) and that "love between man and man is impossible because there must not be sexual intercourse and friendship between man and woman is impossible because there must be sexual intercourse" (Joyce 2000: 86), he falls back into self-alienation and victimizes the only person who could have understood and saved him through her compassion and affection. Duffy's belief that "love between man and man is impossible because there must not be sexual intercourse" embodies his sexual lamentation. While on the one hand, it can be understood as a reference to Duffy's homosexual tendency which further contributes to the description of the character as narcissistic, for again according to the controversial Freudian view narcissism and homosexuality are strongly connected, on the other hand it also accounts for the young man's final rejection of Mrs. Sinico and thereby of the pressure of a societal heteronormativity that compels him to repress his sexual identity. Yet, ignored by her husband and rejected by her lover, Mrs. Sinico embodies the case of women victimized by the male world they live in. And even though Mrs. Sinico has "crossed the line" (Joyce 2000: 87) both metaphorical and physical, she is to be exonerated. It is also worth mentioning that Emily Sinico's death is announced through the newspaper (see Joyce 2000: 86-88), therefore reported with a journalistic objectivity (namely in a detached way, focusing on the facts), which points to Joyce's criticism of the individualistic society of the time, and echoes Virginia Woolf's mentioning of Mrs. Ramsay's death in *To the Lighthouse*. Then the testimonies of the authority figures such as the railway officials and doctors who claim, "No blame attached to anyone" (Joyce 2000: 88) not only exonerate the railway company but also the victim herself. The release of Mrs. Sinico's tragic death in the newspaper constitutes an important *dénouement* in the story. When Duffy, first reads about his ex-lover's death, his visceral cold-heartedness and selfishness is reiterated, since he thought that "not merely had she degraded herself; she had degraded him" (Joyce 2000: 88). Clearly, Duffy thinks of himself as the primary victim in this tragedy, which again shows his lack of empathy, thus contrasting with Emily's ability as a narcissistic mother to love others. But then in a second phase, when Mrs. Sinico makes a ghostly apparition, Duffy seems to undergo a self-examination which leads him to experiencing a feeling of guilt. Mrs. Sinico's spectral apparition could be seen as the reiteration of this mother's narcissistic features, which even after death still strongly influence her former lover emotionally, keeping him in a state of dependency. This idea reminds us of Stephen Dedalus in Joyce's *Ulysses* who is also haunted by his dead mother. DeVault confirms that his perceptions that "he thought her hand touched his" and that "at moments he seemed to feel her voice touch his ear [and] her hand touch his…establish a posthumous mental connection between Duffy and Mrs. Sinico that could provide the opportunity for him to affirm her otherness" (DeVault 2010: 87). Feeling ill at ease, Duffy "asked himself what else he could have done" (Joyce 2000: 89). He wonders "why he had withheld life from her? Why had he sentenced her to death? He felt his moral nature falling to pieces" (ibd.). The series of rhetorical questions reveal Duffy's troubled consciousness, which leads to his awareness of his own loneliness:

> He gnawed the rectitude of his life; he felt that he had been outcast from life's feast. One human being had seemed to love him and he had denied her life and happiness: he had sentenced her to ignominy, a death of shame. He knew that the prostrate creatures down by the wall were watching him and wished him gone. No one wanted him; he was outcast from life's feast. (Joyce 2000: 89-90)

The repetition of the phrase "outcast from life's feast" shows that Duffy is slowly starting to realize that he has been missing out on what life has to offer. Therefore, Emily Sinico's death acts as an epiphany for Duffy, whose manifestation of emotional distress suggests the re-establishment of communication between his surroundings and himself. The final note of the story which reads as follows: "He felt that he was alone" (Joyce 2000: 90) offers a silver lining to Duffy's predicament, and at the same time it provides an elevating portrayal of the mother figure whose death can be read as an altruistic act. This benevolent act affects Duffy. It brings him to reflect on his actual condition and perhaps paradoxically to adopt a more empathic stance.

Contrarily to the critics who argued that James Joyce uses extreme images of women as either virgins or whores, denying them the roundness of actual individuals, these short stories, namely "A Boarding House", "A Mother" and "A Painful Case" prove that through the puzzle-like portrayal of his mother figures, Joyce demands from his readers to bring the bits and pieces together, inviting them to consider the silences, absences, and images which reveal the psychological depth he bestows upon the female characters of *Dubliners*. Since these mothers are depicted as manipulative, selfish and narcissistic, it is easy to immediately negatively criticize and condemn them. However, at the end Joyce seems to exonerate his mothers, by pointing out how the socio-economic and socio-political situation at the time contributes to shaping and sustaining their narcissistic injury. Joyce strategically sets these figures in public places such as boarding houses, concert houses or parades, which are revealed to function as microcosms of Dublin, for these public places gather people from different social classes. Narcissistic mothers in *Dubliners* turn out to function as 'looking-glasses' which mirror the faults and vices of the Irish society, so as to bring changes in the community, for indeed, *Dubliners* was written at a time when Ireland was seeking independence from Great Britain and when Irish nationalism was at its peak. Consequently, even if Joyce does not explicitly refer to this analogy between the motherland and mother figures in the three short stories analysed in this chapter, it is nonetheless still inevitable to read his representation of narcissistic mothers as the embodiment of the conflictual relationship between the motherland (Great Britain) and its dominion (Ireland). The relationship between mother and daughter is characterized by maternal domination over the child's subjectivity and its growing desire for independence, but it also refers to the intricate relation between "mother Ireland", to use Kevin Oheix's word, and its inhabitants. Moreover, Joyce confesses in his letter to Grant Richards: "my intention was to write a chapter of the moral history of my country and I chose Dublin for the scene because that city seemed to me the centre of paralysis" (Johnson 2000: xvii), thus reasserting his desire through *Dubliners* to cast light on society's ills so as to enable individuals' recovery. Therefore, the examination of Joyce's short stories reveals the writer's socio-political engagement and shows a clear interconnection between the representation of narcissism and the political situation of the time, an interdependence which is further reflected through Virginia Woolf's criticism of the Great War in *To the Lighthouse* and Jean Rhys' virulent denunciation of the rise of fascism in *Good Morning, Midnight.*

5 A Mother's 'Divided Self' in Virginia Woolf's *To the Lighthouse*

> "About life, about death; about Mrs Ramsay."
>
> *(Woolf 2006: 146)*

This thought expressed by the artist Lily Briscoe, beautifully encapsulates Virginia Woolf's novel *To the Lighthouse*, by positioning the mother figure, Mrs. Ramsay, at the centre of the novel. It reflects how she sees herself and how she is also perceived by the other characters who seem to revolve around her. In her work, Woolf establishes a portrayal of Mrs. Ramsay as a narcissistic mother and demonstrates that if at times her protagonist shows signs of self-absorption and is constantly on the lookout for self-enhancement opportunities, she is nonetheless still capable of loving and caring for her family. Thus, she demonstrates that love for one's self does not necessarily exclude love for others. Her narcissistic features are revealed to act as a shield and are a means for self-preservation. They allow her to work around the rigid values of Victorian society by enhancing her feeling of self-worth and thereby, protecting her from losing sight of her own self. The novel also considers another aspect of narcissism, which culminates in the writer's criticism of the Great War. This is especially vivid in the section *Time Passes*. Through her depiction of oppressive male characters, who stand for tyrannical rulers, Woolf denounces patriarchy and the threat it represents. Her idea of patriarchy constitutes a major difference with Freud who saw this authority as an optimal order but ended up disillusioned by the coming of the Second World War. Despite their substantial differences, Julia Briggs observes that "Freud and Woolf shared many values and common experiences; they belonged to and were the products of the same cultural moment" (Briggs 2011: para. 2). Although she claimed that she resisted Freud's ideas, Woolf who met the man for the first time at 20 Maresfield Gardens in 1939, was clearly influenced by his works. If she only encountered him personally in 1939, evidence that she was exposed to his theories much earlier exist, for instance, through the Hogarth Press, which became the official English representor of the 'International Psychoanalytical Library', publisher of Freud's work. She admits: "I have not studied Dr Freud or any psychoanalyst – indeed I think I have never read any of their books: my knowledge is merely from superficial talk. Therefore, any use of their methods must be instinctive" (Woolf 1975: 36). This has prompted critics to read *To the Lighthouse* through a Freudian lens, especially in their interpretation of Woolf's description of family bonds, which as this chapter shows, is of great significance in the analysis of Mrs. Ramsay. Previous critical discourse on the character of Mrs. Ramsay indicates that she has been widely regarded flatteringly as "unquestionably one of the most perfect statements of feminine sensibility, intuition, and maternal comfort in literature, as a magnetic force, entering and irradiating the lives of those around her" (Proudfit 1971: 26). She was also understood as an idealized vision of wife and mother, as a symbol of life's victory over death and as a model of perfection. Brenda Silver explains that some critics such as Joseph Blotner suggested that "Woolf's concept of woman's role in life is crystallized in the character of Mrs. Ramsay, whose attributes are those of major female figures in pagan myth" (Silver 2009: 261), for instance as mother (Rhea), Mrs. Ramsay is the perfect embodiment of the nurturing and benevolent mother, as wife (Demeter) she stands for fertility and sensuality. Yet, traces of counter interpretation to Mrs. Ramsay's idealized portrayal, although less common, still exist. For example, Glenn Pedersen, by underlining Mrs. Ramsay's ambivalent portrayal, argues that if at first she superficially seems to be a "beautiful and positive creature" (Pedersen 1958: 585), she is gradually revealed to be a negative force which hinders the integration of the family while she lives. Pedersen understands the journey to the lighthouse as a way for the other members of the family to overcome the domination of an absolute matriarch, "a dominion that lives ten years beyond her Self" (ibd.). This mixed reception of Mrs. Ramsay does not only underline Woolf's conflicting feelings toward her own mother, but it also shows that it is no longer possible to think of Mrs. Ramsay either as flawless mother and wife, or solely as destructive power. If critics have disagreed on the protagonist's good intentions, they seem to have unanimously acknowledged Mrs. Ramsay's physical attractiveness as "the perfection of Greek beauty" (Bradbury 1994: viii).

5.1 A 'BLUNDERED' PORTRAYAL OF MRS. RAMSAY

5.1.1 Mrs. Ramsay: A Charismatic Woman

Mrs. Ramsay's physical perfection is suggested through the implicit analogy to a work of art, as the narrative demonstrates. By delaying the character's description, Woolf gives the impression that the reader is stopping in front of a painting in order to contemplate the beauty that emanates from it. This idea is, for instance, illustrated through the reference to Charles Tansley's observation: "all at once he realized that it was this: it was this: – she was the most beautiful person he had ever seen" (Woolf 2006: 15), a remark which comes as a conclusion to a detailed description of his hostess' physical appearance. This comparison between Mrs. Ramsay's beauty and art is confirmed later on in the novel through Lily's attempt to capture Mrs. Ramsay in her painting and hence, by doing so, immortalizing her beauty. Further evidence is reflected through her power of seduction on the male audience, for example, as William Bankes watches Mrs. Ramsay, Lily remarks that "for him to gaze [...] at Mrs Ramsay was a rapture, equivalent [...] to the loves of dozen of young men" (Woolf 2006: 41). However, her power of seduction does not only reside in her physical beauty but also in the image of nurturing mother that she conveys as Lily's observation of Mr. Bankes points out: "the world by all means should have shared it, could Mr. Bankes have said why that woman pleased him so; why the sight of her reading a fairy tale to her boy had upon him precisely the same effect as the solution of a scientific problem, so that he rested in contemplation of it..." (Woolf 2006: 41). Here, an analogy between the satisfaction of solving a "scientific problem" and the pleasure of observing Mrs. Ramsay as she performs her role of mother is established. This connection between the logical precision and the image of mother-son relationship is reminiscent of the iconic representation and celebration of motherhood in the work of Michael Angelo, as it is explicitly referred to in the text (see Woolf 2006: 27-28) later on. Thereby, it reiterates this idea of beauty as art, at the same time as it suggests a sexualized image of the mother through the acknowledgment of her fertility. This effigy-like description of Mrs. Ramsay guarantees the posterity and permanence of her beauty, for as Mr. Ramsay full of admiration notes, his wife "was astonishingly beautiful. Her beauty seemed to him, if that were possible, to increase" (Woolf 2006: 98). Mrs. Ramsay also possesses the ability to turn an "odious little man" (Woolf 2006: 16) like Charles Tansley into a gentleman, by making him feel "many things, something in particular that excited him and disturbed him for reasons which he could not give" (Woolf 2006: 13). And through the use of an omniscient narrator, Tansley's desire to impress his hostess is put forward: "he would like her to see him, gowned and hooded, walking in a procession. A fellowship, a professorship – he felt capable of anything and saw himself ..." (ibd.). His attempt to impress Mrs. Ramsay is brought to light, first by showing good manners when he insists on carrying her bag, then by his desire to show off his knowledge in the hope of sparking her admiration and respect for him. Finally, his fascination for Mrs. Ramsay is indicated when he acknowledges being "under the influence of that extraordinary emotion which had been growing all the walk, had begun in the garden when he had wanted to take her bag, had increased in the town when he had wanted to tell her everything about himself" (Woolf 2006: 15). Under her spell, he admits that "he was coming to see himself and everything he had ever known gone crooked a little" (ibd.). The use of words such as "growing", "increased" and "everything" gradually shows an intensification in Tansley's feeling for Mrs. Ramsay, which culminates with the sexually loaded image of everything...gone crooked", reinforced by Tansley noticing "a man digging in a drain stopped digging and looked at her; let his arm fall down and looked at her" (Woolf 2006: 15). As a result, it makes Charles Tansley feels "an extraordinary pride; felt the wind and the cyclamen and the violets for he was walking with a beautiful woman for the first time in his life. He had hold of her bag" (ibd.). This previous scene indicates Mrs. Ramsay's ability to empower men with a feeling of pride, at the same time as she is capable of softening their hearts as Charles' sudden awareness of the flowers indicates, and even of emasculating them as the symbolical drooping of the worker's arm suggests. Mrs. Ramsay's physical attractiveness is mainly visible through the male characters' reaction. The narrative also indicates that she is well-aware of her power of seduction: "She bore about with her, she could not help knowing it, the torch of her beauty; she carried it erect into any room that she entered" (Woolf 2006: 36) and she responds to it with excessive pride. Through third-person narration, her self-satisfaction and her narcissism are stressed: "She had been admired. She had been loved. She had entered rooms where mourners sat. Tears had flown in her presence. Men, and women too, letting go the multiplicity of things, had allowed themselves with her the relief of simplicity" (ibd.). This passage is key to several essential aspects of Mrs. Ramsay's personality. Compared to a figure of the monarchy, she is described as holding "the torch of her beauty erect" as she enters the room, making a remarkable entrance wherever she goes and causing people to shed tears in her presence. This hyperbolic description parallels her excessive sense of pride and grandiosity. It also constitutes a subtle reference to the powerful Britannia, the female personification of Britain who is often represented armed with Poseidon's trident and wearing her Corinthian helmet. Thus, a first connection between mother figures and motherland is established. Simultaneously, it echoes the ambiguous feelings towards the British Empire, whose grandeur and triumphalism were already questioned in the last decades of the Victorian period. Besides, it is with a hint of irony that Woolf reveals Mrs. Ramsay's inappropriate satisfaction at the thought of being loved and admired. She writes that "(here insensibly she drew herself together, physically, the sense of her own beauty becoming, as it did seldom, present to her)" (Woolf 2006: 36). These words are written between parentheses and represent the writer's ironical voice, reinforced by the extensive hyperbolic use of the lexical field of royalty. If at first, she seems to imply that Mrs. Ramsay hardly ever thinks of herself as attractive, she rapidly and in the same passage, depicts her protagonist as she is pleasantly contemplating her beauty. The image of humbleness she mirrors at first is gradually deconstructed, casting light on her false humility and concealed self-absorption. While this passage reveals Mrs. Ramsay's narcissistic self, the reference to her queen-like demeanour reiterates Woolf's desire to present her protagonist's beauty according to the Ruskinian pre-Raphaelite aesthetics. In accordance with Ruskin's notorious idealization of the queen whose "intellect is not for invention or creation, but for sweet ordering, arrangement, and decision" (Vadillo 2015: 127). This is precisely how Woolf depicts Mrs. Ramsay, as someone who is less of an intellectual but whose duty is primarily to manage the household: "she thought, possibly she might have managed things better – her husband; money; his books. But for her own part she would never for a single second regret her decision, evade difficulties, or slur over duties" (Woolf 2006: 9). Ana Parejo Vadillo notes that Mrs. Ramsay is "the generous hostess that excels at arranging dinner parties" (Vadillo 2015: 127). She also admirably makes her guests "feel at ease with her judicious praising" (ibd.). These dinner parties she organizes are also a way for her to create opportunities for self-enhancement, a chance to put herself forward by presenting her best profile. Her apparition at dinner is again described in majestic terms:

> And, like some queen who finding her people gathered in the hall, looks down upon them, and descends among them, and acknowledges their tributes silently, and accepts their devotion and their prostration before her (Paul did not move a muscle but looked straight before him as she passed), she went down, and crossed the hall and bowed her head very slightly, as if she accepted what they could not say: their tribute to her beauty. (Woolf 2006: 68)

Contrarily to the earlier quotation (see Woolf 2006: 36), here an explicit reference to Mrs. Ramsay's regal-like attitude is provided. This is underlined by her ceremonious walk and her haughty bow, reinforced by her "look[ing] *down upon*" her guests, who are referred to as "*her people*" (*my emphasis*), thereby creating a feeling of distance between them. Woolf's dexterous use of exaggeration is fabulously effective in revealing Mrs. Ramsay's ambivalent nature. If in the previous passage, Mrs. Ramsay appears to be self-confident and in a position of power, she nonetheless later on cannot help feeling threatened by younger women, such as Minta Doyle and admits that "for a moment she felt what she had never expected to feel again – jealousy. For he, her husband, felt it too – Minta's glow; he likes these girls" (Woolf 2006: 81). Alarmed by the signs of ageing, she is concerned about her physical appearance and acknowledges that "indeed she was not jealous, only now and then, when she made herself look in her glass, a little resentful that she had grown old, perhaps, by her own fault" (ibd.). And as a response to the threat to her self-esteem, Mrs. Ramsay decides and requires that "Paul must sit by her" (ibd.). Evidence of her self-centeredness abound in her interaction with her family and guests. Glenn Pedersen observes that her "attitude towards others is determined by their attitude towards her" (Pedersen 1958: 586), a statement which is confirmed when Charles Tansley manifests his admiration for her, leading her to the conclusion that after all she likes him, even if earlier she has expressed her contempt for this "odious little man" (Woolf 2006: 16). She also shows gratitude to Carmichael when she has the impression that he finally liked her: "without knowing why she felt that he liked her better than he had ever done before; and with a feeling of relief and gratitude she returned his bow and passed through the door which he held open for her" (Woolf 2006: 90). Mrs. Ramsay values what people think of her, therefore she makes sure to create a hospitable environment for her guests. Performing her role as exemplary hostess, she "choose[s] a specially tender piece [of meat] for William Bankes" (Woolf 2006: 82). As expected, Bankes immediately reacts positively to his preferential treatment by praising his hostess; "'it is a triumph'" he declares, "it was rich; it was tender. It was perfectly cooked. How did she manage these things in the depths of the country?", he asks her thinking "she was a wonderful woman", making Mrs. Ramsay greatly satisfied, for she knew that "all his reverence had returned" (ibd.). Contrarily to the male guests who were all very impressed by her generosity and sense of hospitality, Lily is critical of Mrs. Ramsay's "childlike" behaviour and thinks "how absurd she was, sitting up there with all her beauty opened again in her, talking about the skins of vegetables. There was something frightening about her. She was irresistible" (Woolf 2006: 82). Since she follows Victorian etiquette closely, Mrs. Ramsay's sense of hospitality is praised by her guests. However, the narration, by granting access to Lily's thoughts reveals the flip side of the coin. With a series of antitheses, such as "to triumph and to mock" or "frightening" and "irresistible" (ibd.), Mrs. Ramsay's ambivalent nature is confirmed. Later on, Woolf subtly refers to the psychological complexity of her protagonist and thereby, to the existence of a darker side (here, her narcissistic self), which she hides from others. Carolyn Dever confirms that "Through 'a wedge-shaped core of darkness' reminiscent of the triangular purple blur in Lily's painting, Mrs. Ramsay achieves access to a self that has little to do with that which is lost to her family and friends following her death" (Dever 1998: 205). Indeed, if at first Mrs. Ramsay seems to conform to Victorian decorum and to the image of 'Angel in the House', rapidly it becomes clear that her self-centeredness is a means for self-preservation. Dever understands "Mrs. Ramsay's interiority as well as her private adventure story" as an attempt from Woolf to "challenge those conventions of genre so consistently articulated through the mother's containment" (Dever 1998: 205). If many critics have chosen to see Mrs. Ramsay as 'Angel in the House', she is however never referred as such in the text, contrarily to Prue (Mrs. Ramsay's daughter) who is described as "a perfect angel with the others, and sometimes now, at night especially, she took one's breath away with her beauty" (Vadillo 2015: 129). Woolf intentionally never refers directly to Mrs. Ramsay as an angel because even if her protagonist staunchly advocates the traditional Victorian idea of marriage, she does not entirely comply with the social norms. While Victorian etiquette demands that women be "a perfect angel with the others" (Woolf 2006: 49), Mrs. Ramsay's good deeds are not completely selfless.

5.1.2 Shadows on Mrs. Ramsay's Good Deeds

In the opening scene of the novel, Mrs. Ramsay is pictured knitting a pair of stockings for the lighthouse keeper's son, who suffers from tuberculosis. While this passage shows her compassionate nature, it also subtly discloses this mother's cryptic personality. Putting herself in others' shoes, she imagines how it would feel like to be trapped "for a whole month at a time, and possibly more in stormy weather, upon a rock the size of a tennis lawn" (Woolf 2006: 8). And as a self-respecting mother, she tries to instil moral righteousness in her daughters by raising their awareness of the unfortunate reality of others. She asked them: "how would you like that? […] if you were married, not to see your wife, not to know how your children were; […] to see the same dreary waves breaking week after week, and then a dreadful storm coming, and the windows covered with spray, and birds dashed against the lamp […]" (ibd.). Here, the repetition of the second-person pronoun 'you' and the use of a series of rhetorical questions turn Mrs.

Ramsay's reflection on other's fate into a sermon. It underlines her religious devotion and the importance she gives to moral values. Then, her dramatized ideas of life on "a rock the size of a tennis lawn" reveal her ability to give free reign to her imagination when it serves her purpose and demonstrates that her benevolence is far from being disinterested. As the novel progresses, it is made obvious that she expects admiration and applause from those she helps and treats with generosity. Again, this confirms her need and her ability to find opportunities to shine. Carmichael's thoughts on Mrs. Ramsay contribute to this idea. He suspects "that all this desire of hers to give, to help, was vanity" (Woolf 2006: 36-37). He is equally convinced that she expects "that people might say of her: 'O Mrs Ramsay! dear Mrs Ramsay ... Mrs Ramsay, of course!' and need her and send for her and admire her?" (Woolf 2006: 37). Mrs. Ramsay's altruistic gestures are not only discredited, but Lily also believes that she detects problems where there are none and is persuaded that Mrs. Ramsay's pity for William Bankes "was one of those misjudgements of hers that seemed to be instinctive and to arise from some need of her own rather than of other people's" (Woolf 2006: 70). Lily is of the opinion that Mr. Bankes "is not in the least pitiable. He has his work" (ibd.). Therefore, Mrs. Ramsay seems to find pleasure when she feels that others need her and that she is indispensable to their happiness. Thus, Mrs. Ramsay's maternal benevolence can be questioned. In fact, she has once been accused of "robbing a mother from her daughter's affections" and was blamed for her "wishing to dominate, wishing to interfere, making people do what she wished" (Woolf 2006: 49). Of this charge against her, Mrs. Ramsay "thought it most unjust" (ibd.). Yet, it is through her relationship with her children and Lily, who acts as a substitute daughter, that her narcissism is best epitomized.

5.2 BEHIND SELF-LOVE LURKS THE LOVE FOR OTHERS

5.2.1 A Narcissistic Mother who wishes her children well

Confessing that "she never wanted James to grow a day older or Cam either [...] never to see them grow up into long-legged monsters" (Woolf 2006: 49), Mrs. Ramsay shows that it is within her function as mother that she feels most valuable. She wishes for her children what she desires for herself, namely happiness and affection. Thus, she tries to instill her principles in them, for she is convinced of their benefits. As a result, she teaches them respect for others, for instance when she forbids her children to mock Charles Tansley and when she insists that they offer assistance to those who are in need. But above all she attempts to instil her conservative principles into those in her surroundings, mainly her obsession with marriage. She is convinced that "people must marry; people must have children" (Woolf 2006: 51). Taking her role of matchmaker seriously, she sends Minta Doyle and Paul Rayley on a walk after luncheon, persuaded that "they will be perfectly happy" (ibd.) together. But Mrs. Ramsay still demonstrates that she favours her own children's happiness over her friends', and it is through her relationship with her daughter that this idea is best illustrated. Prue appears to have much in common with her mother. First and foremost, her beauty is underlined on several occasions in the novel, as if it is one of her main characteristics. Then, Mrs. Ramsay's love for her daughter is visible through her desire to see Prue be much happier than Minta. She thinks: "You will be as happy as she is one of these days. You will be much happier, she added, because you are my daughter, she meant; her own daughters must be happier than other people's daughters" (Woolf 2006: 89). So, accordingly, a couple of months later, the reader learns that "[Prue Ramsay, leaning on her father's arm was given in marriage that May. What people said, could have been more fitting? And, they added, how beautiful she looked!]" (Woolf

2006: 108). Here, brackets are used to report the happy event. These punctuations are usually used to separate off information that is not essential from the rest of the sentence. This deliberate choice on the writer's part suggests that Prue's wedding should not come as a surprise to the reader, for as the narrator warns: "always she [Mrs. Ramsay] got her own way in the end" (Woolf 2006: 82). While on the one hand, Prue's wedding reasserts Mrs. Ramsay's triumph, on the other hand, the event succinctly reported echoes Prue's ephemeral happiness, since "[Prue Ramsay died that summer in some illness connected with childbirth, which was indeed a tragedy, people said. They said nobody deserved happiness more.]" (Woolf 2006: 108). Not only are the similarities between Mrs. Ramsay and Prue reflected through their physical resemblance but they are also expressed through their personal journey through marriage and then later, through death, which is strategically announced in similar fashion. Mrs. Ramsay's death is also communicated abruptly, within brackets: "[Mr Ramsay stumbling along a passage stretched his arms out one dark morning, but Mrs Ramsay having died rather suddenly the night before, he stretched his arms out. They remained empty]" (Woolf 2006: 105). However, if Mrs. Ramsay can be criticized for sustaining an archaic vision of marriage, she is nonetheless praised for her motherly affection and devotion. Prue responds to her mother's tenderness positively: "'That's my mother,' thought Prue. Yes; Minta should look at her; Paul Rayley should look at her. That is the thing itself, she felt, as if there were only one person like that in the world; her mother" (Woolf 2006: 94). Full of admiration and affection for her mother, Prue indicates the existence of a possessive love which unites mother and daughter. This is suggested through the use of the adjective "my" in her insistent and positive affirmation "That's *my* mother" (*my emphasis*), then reinforced by the daughter's wish to remain a child and "never leave home" (Woolf 2006: 94). Prue's statement echoes Mrs. Ramsay's own earlier desire "never to see them [her children] grow up into long-legged monsters" (Woolf 2006: 49).

This narcissistic mother is also very protective of her children. She tries to protect James from harsh reality. She knew that "this going to the Lighthouse was a passion of his" (Woolf 2006: 16) and is infuriated by her husband and Charles Tansley's lack of consideration for the child's feeling. She thinks: "as if her husband had not said enough, with his caustic saying that it would not be fine tomorrow, this odious little man went and rubbed it in all over again" (ibd.). Then, she protects Cam against the scary skull hanging on the wall in the children's bedroom. As a compassionate mother, she encourages her daughter to use her imagination to think of the scary skull as "a nice black pig like the pigs at the farm" (Woolf 2006: 93), but when she realizes that her first approach does not work, she uses her shawl to hide the skull, which gains her the child's gratitude. This scene is essential in drawing a portrait of a nurturing mother, as it captures Mrs. Ramsay in a moment of intimacy with her daughter: "she came back to Cam and laid her head almost flat on the pillow beside Cam's" (ibd.). Comforting her daughter with her poetic imagination, she "said how lovely it looked now, how the fairies would love it" (ibd.), hence revealing that even if she sometimes appears to be self-centered, her emotions are far from being thwarted when it comes to her children. In fact, part of being a narcissistic mother involves being proud of her children. This aspect is reflected when she thinks of James as "the most gifted, the most sensitive of her children" and of Prue as "a perfect angel with her beauty" (Woolf 2006: 49). She admits that Andrew's "gift for mathematics was extraordinary" and that Nancy and Roger "were both wild creatures now" (ibd.). She acknowledges Rose's "wonderful gift with her hands" (ibd.) and as for Jasper, she did not like that he "should shoot birds" (Woolf 2006: 50). But she believes "it was only a stage; they all went through stages" (ibd.). From Mrs. Ramsay's thoughts on her children's talents and behaviour, it is made evident that she recognizes the good qualities in each of them. Her pride can be linked to her sense of achievement in her children's education, for which she accepts full responsibility. She marks an important contrast with her husband, who endorses the function of dutiful father, rather than of a passionate one.

Described as "stop[ping] to light his pipe, looked once at his wife and son in the window" (Woolf 2006: 30), Mr. Ramsay's position suggests his physical distance from the rest of the family, which also parallels his emotional aloofness from his children. "Fortified and satisfied" (ibd.) by this sight, he complies with his role as breadwinner, which allows him to focus on his intellectual work. He appears to be rather content with his present familial situation and his intellectual activity. He confesses being "for the most part happy; he had his wife; he had his children; he had promised in six weeks to talk nonsense to the young men of Cardiff about Locke, Hume, Berkeley and the causes of French Revolution" (Woolf 2006: 39). His withdrawal from his role as father reinforces his wife's opportunity in raising the children according to her own principles. This results in some obvious similarities between mother and daughters. For example, Rose's sewing skills remind us of Mrs. Ramsay's ability to knit stockings, or her children's habit of exaggeration which she acknowledges, "they had from her" (Woolf 2006: 9). The father's disengagement from the children's education starkly contributes to deepening the mother's connection with her children. In fact, this is a recurrent motif in the novels and short stories examined in this book.

5.2.2 Pleading not guilty for the hostilities between father and son

However, if Mrs. Ramsay is seen as nurturing, she has also been identified as a negative force which prevents her children from bonding with their father while she lives, and she has been held accountable for the tensions between James (at that time six years old) and Mr. Ramsay. By declaring that the family's journey to the lighthouse will not take place due to bad weather conditions, this father has aroused his son's anger: "had there been an axe handy, a poker, or any weapon that would have gashed a hole in his father's breast and killed him, there and then, James would have seized it" (Woolf 2006: 7). These words underline the son's Oedipal feeling. They attest to James' rage and violence of emotion towards the man who "standing [...] lean as a knife, narrow as the blade of one [...] grins sarcastically" and is "pleased with disillusioning his son and casting ridicule upon his wife" (ibd.). The child's Oedipus complex is conveyed, on the one hand through his wish to kill his father and on the other hand, through his strong attachment to his mother who "was ten thousand times better than he [the father] was (James thought)" (ibd.). Here, the use of parenthesis implies that we are granted access to James' mind or unconscious thoughts. The reference to the child's age adds to the Oedipal reading of the character, since according to the Freudian standard, the child's desire for the parent of the opposite sex occurs during the 'phallic stage' (the third stage of the five psychosexual development stages), which corresponds to the ages of three to six. The rivalry between father and son over the mother is established through the comparison of Mr. Ramsay to a "lean knife", which symbolically represents an erect phallus. It is also used in Woolf's novel *Mrs. Dalloway,* essentially in Peter Walsh's description and points at his needy and overbearing bahaviour. In *To the Lighthouse,* the image of the knife reveals the sexual undertones which permeate James' thoughts, whose perception of his father indicates the emotional and physical threat that he embodies in his son's eyes. Also, the third-person narrative insists on James' rejection of the father in favour of the mother's company: "he hated him [Mr. Ramsay] for coming up to them, for stopping and looking down on them; he hated him for interrupting them; he hated him for the exaltation and sublimity of his gestures; for the magnificence of his head; for his exactingness and egotism" (Woolf 2006: 33). In the previous quotation, the anaphoric use of "he hated him" insists on James' hostility to his father. Then, the exclusive use of the personal pronouns 'he' and 'them' unravels the son's longing for a fusional and exclusive relationship with the mother. This idea is made clear in: "but most of all he hated the twang and twitter of his father's emotion which, vibrating round them, disturbed the perfect simplicity and good sense of his relations with his mother" (ibd.). Since in this scene, the narration focuses on James' opinions and Oedipus complex, the mother is discharged from having any responsibility in estranging the son from the father. In fact, no passage in the novel clearly suggests that Mrs. Ramsay intentionally attempted to undermine the relationship between the children and their father, by encouraging a symbiotic relationship. In fact, it is quite the opposite. James is the one who possessively requests his mother's full attention and is disturbed by his father's presence. Therefore, he wishes that "by looking fixedly at the page, he hoped to make him move on" and "by pointing his finger at a word, he hoped to recall his mother's attention, which, he knew angrily, wavered instantly his father stopped" (Woolf 2006: 33). James' Oedipus complex can be considered an essential stage in the child's development process, and his love for his mother and hatred for his father as a result of his personal conflict. Thus, it suggests that Mrs. Ramsay cannot be blamed for her son's rejection of the father. This is made evident when at the end of the novel, James "only now, as he grew older" (Woolf 2006: 150) realizes that "it was not him, that old man reading whom he wanted to kill, but it was the thing that descended on him" (Woolf 2006: 151). Consequently, neither Mrs. Ramsay nor Mr. Ramsay is responsible for James' "impotent rage" (Woolf 2006: 150). Furthermore, capturing the image of a man "demanding sympathy" (Woolf 2006: 34), the portrait of the father as tyrant is deconstructed. He demonstrates signs of vulnerability and fragility, while his wife depicted as "flashing her needles, confident, upright" (Woolf 2006: 33) occupies a position of power. Overwhelmed by his constant demands to be nurtured and reassured, Mrs. Ramsay uses her son as a buffer against her invasive husband: "standing stiff between her knees", James felt "the arid scimitar of the father, the egotistical man, plunged and smote, demanding sympathy" (Woolf 2006: 34). Here, Mrs. Ramsay's superiority over her husband is reasserted. She uses her position as a mother to protect herself from the demanding husband. Then, James' position, erect between his mother's knees evokes this idea of a love triangle between mother, father and son, which is best depicted through Lily's painting of a purple colour triangle representing "Mrs Ramsay reading to James" (Woolf, 2006: 45). To this representation, William Bankes reacts sceptically and wonders how "mother and child then – objects of universal veneration, and in this case the mother was famous for her beauty – might be reduced, he pondered, to a purple shadow without irreverence" (ibd.). On the one hand, the purple triangle can be read as a reference to James' illicit sexual desire for the mother, on the other hand, it reveals Lily's difficulty in successfully "connect[ing] this mass on the right hand with that on the left" (Woolf 2006: 46) without destroying the unity of the whole portrait. Thus, it can also be interpreted as a reflection of the artist's own personal conflict.

5.2.3 "About life, about death, about Lily Briscoe"

Lily Briscoe's relationship with Mrs. Ramsay is similar to one between mother and daughter and as the narration points out, it was "unity that she [Lily] desired" (Woolf 2006: 44). It was "intimacy itself... she had thought, leaning her head on Mrs Ramsay's knee" (ibd.) that she was looking for. This image echoes the "intimacy" between James and Mrs. Ramsay and reminds us of Michael Angelo's portrayal of the iconographic mother and child. Lily's longing for the maternal figure is suggested in the novel through omission. While details are given about her father, whom she left for Mrs. Ramsay's company, the silence around Lily's biological mother constitutes a cue, which points at her quest for the lost mother through her desire to bond with Mrs. Ramsay. Subsequently, Mrs. Ramsay demonstrates motherly affection and tenderness for Lily who she loves as her own daughter and as an extension of herself. She wishes that Lily would marry Mr. Bankes. She believes that "they have so many things in common. Lily is fond of flowers. They are both cold and aloof and rather self-sufficing" (Woolf 2006: 85). Consequently, she makes a point to "arrange for them to take a long walk together" (ibd.). Although Lily seems to be the exact opposite of Mrs. Ramsay, for example, she rejects the ideas of marriage and family that Mrs. Ramsay fiercely advocates, she is nonetheless revealed to have very much in common with her, especially in the way they treat men. Remembering how Charles Tansley sneered, claiming that "women can't paint, women can't write" (Woolf 2006: 42), Lily Briscoe cannot help despising the man. However, she still shows sign of empathy for him and tries to make the latter feel comfortable by engaging into a conversation with him. She believes that "there is a code of behaviour [...], whose seventh article (it may be) says that on occasion of this sort it behoves the woman, whatever her own occupation might be, to go to the help of the young man opposite so that he may expose and relieve the thigh bones, the ribs, of his vanity" (Woolf 2006: 74-75). Lily's previous thought underlines her awareness of Victorian decorum. When she invites him to join the trip to the lighthouse (see Woolf 2006: 75), her proposition is similar to Mrs. Ramsay's charitable offer to "the odious little man" (Woolf 2006: 12) to accompany her on her errands. In fact, these two scenes are very alike. Both women adopt a similar approach. First, they flatter Charles Tansley's ego, then expect his chivalrous zeal: Lily imagines being rescued from fire and Mrs. Ramsay anticipates that he would carry her bag. Although Lily advocates independence for women, she has nevertheless internalized social expectation and complies with the old-fashioned etiquettes, which Mrs. Ramsay has primarily embodied. As she recognizes in her protégé some common features, Mrs. Ramsay proves to narcissistically love Lily. She also admires Lily's independence and originality. She admits that "there was in Lily a thread of something; a flare of something; something of her own which Mrs Ramsay liked very much indeed" (Woolf 2006: 85). As for Lily, her extreme affection for Mrs. Ramsay is expressed through her difficulty "to control her impulse to fling herself (thank heaven she had always resisted so far) at Mrs Ramsay's knee and say to her – but what could one say to her? 'I'm in love with you?'" (Woolf 2006: 19). Her love and her admiration for Mrs. Ramsay are subdued by her awareness of the mother's vanity and self-centeredness. Similarly to James' biased criticism of his father, Lily's negative judgment of Mrs. Ramsay is influenced by the artist's own issues to come to terms with the pain that the absence of her biological mother has generated and who she tries to replace through her relationship with Mrs. Ramsay. She is constantly seeking validations of her achievement from the substitute mother, for example, she is satisfied when she realizes that by being nice to Charles Tansley, she has pleased her hostess, or she feels hurt when she realizes that "Mrs Ramsay cared not a fig for her painting" (Woolf 2006: 43). Lily longs for symbiosis with the mother and is tortured by her desire to unite with Mrs. Ramsay as the following statement emphasizes: "What device for becoming, like waters poured into one jar, inextricably the same, one with the object one adored? Could the body achieve it, or the mind, subtly mingling in the intricate passages of the brain? Or the heart? Could loving, as people called it, make her and Mrs Ramsay one?" (Woolf 2006: 44). Here again, Mrs. Ramsay's voice is silenced and therefore in a way this suggests that she is not responsible for encouraging and supporting Lily's fusional love. However, it is essentially through Lily's struggle to bring her painting to completion that her personal conflict is embodied. Her work can be regarded as a representation of her own self and as a reflection of her psychological struggle both as a female artist and a woman who has been deprived of maternal ministrations. She dreads showing it to others because it would mean exposing herself to an external gaze. She would rather prefer "snatch[ing] the picture off the easel" (Woolf 2006: 44) than having someone looking at what she herself describes as "the residue of her thirty-three years, the deposit of each day's living, mixed with something more secret than she had ever spoken or shown in the course of all those days was an agony" (Woolf 2006: 45). Later on, she admits that "the picture was not of them [Mrs. Ramsay and James] ... Or not in his sense", that "there were other senses, too, in which one might reverence them" (ibd.). Lily's acknowledgement that her portrait is not necessarily a representation of Mrs. Ramsay and James proposes another reading of the purple triangle. It posits that it could be the reflection of the young lady's own conflicting relationship with maternal figures who she only briefly encountered. Mrs. Ramsay has been blamed for Lily's thwarted artistic inspiration. In fact, Lily is unable to complete the portrait not only while Mrs. Ramsay is alive but also after her death. The novel has the dynamic of the 'Bildungsroman', since it focuses on Lily's psychological and artistic growth, which is made possible through her relationship with Mrs. Ramsay. The latter's detachment allows Lily to seek reparation for the traumatic loss of her biological mother, whose absence is created by narratorial omission. She is not even mentioned once in the text, while Lily's father is referred twice in the novel. The missing details about the mother represent the painter's unconscious desire to deny painful memories through the defense mechanism of repression. By entering into a mother-daughter relationship with Mrs. Ramsay, Lily is encouraged to gradually work out her mother issues. First, through her ambivalent feelings for her substitute mother (sometimes admiring, sometimes reproving), Lily demonstrates that she is slowly realizing that there is no such thing as an ideal mother and that one can still love and at the same time disagree with her. It is by experiencing her death that she is able to mourn her biological mother. Mrs. Ramsay's death gives her a new chance to grieve. The process of mourning starts with her realization that "she had felt, now she could stand up to Mrs. Ramsay – a tribute to the astonishing power that Mrs Ramsay had over one" (Woolf 2006: 144) and indicates gradual detachment from the mother figure. Then her realization through Mrs. Ramsay's spectral apparition that "to want and not to have" (Woolf 2006: 146) is part of "ordinary experience" (Woolf 2006: 164) casts light on her awareness that death is part of life. This acknowledgement leads her to grab her brush again and "with a sudden intensity, as if she saw it for a second, she drew a line there, in the centre. It was done; it was finished. Yes, she thought, laying down her brush in extreme fatigue, I have had my vision" (Woolf 2006: 170). Mrs. Ramsay appears to function more as a helper than an antagonist in Lily's psychological resolution, which is expressed through her burst of inspiration and the significant "line there, in the centre" reflecting Lily's final detachment from both Mrs. Ramsay and her biological mother. This claim is confirmed by Carolyn Dever who explains that "for the sake of Lily Briscoe's 'vision', aesthetic achievement is predicated on the transition from melancholia to mourning, on the ability to forsake the maternal object as an object"

(Dever 1998: 207). Therefore, Mrs. Ramsay's narcissistic love for Lily Briscoe as well as for her biological children does not prevent her from benevolently caring for them. It is quite the contrary; she is revealed to love them passionately and even if sometimes she makes the wrong decisions when it comes to their education, they do not appear to hold grudges against her. They know that she has their happiness at heart. Consequently, the novel implies that this narcissistic mother is capable of demonstrating love for others and that her self-centeredness acts as a means for self-preservation.

5.3 NARCISSISM AS MEANS FOR SELF-PRESERVATION

5.3.1 Renegotiating Women's Position in Society

Some critics have accused Mrs. Ramsay of being the embodiment of female oppression, since "she has perfectly adopted the roles entrusted to her by tradition" (Yildiz 2013: 19), blindly advocates Victorian ideals of marriage and tries to fulfil the role of 'perfect hostess'. However, even if she is not quite the representation of the 'New Woman' yet, she nonetheless appears to have learnt how to find a way around social pressure, by displaying features, which allows her to strengthen her self-esteem. Again, Mrs. Ramsay is able to make use of Victorian decorum to her advantage. She finds opportunity for self-enhancement, for instance at the dinner party she organizes and through the good deeds she accomplishes. Her narcissistic self becomes a means to escape briefly Victorian oppression. She has learnt to find her way around it and often to turn it to her own advantage. As a wife, she preserves her 'Self' by distancing herself emotionally from her husband, whose constant needs for reassurance and affection have the potential to "wear Mrs Ramsay to death" (Woolf 2006: 23). To Mr. Ramsay's excessive demands for sympathy, his wife does not always respond as he expects: "he wanted something – wanted the thing she always found it so difficult to give him; wanted her to tell him that she loved him. And that, no, she could not do" (Woolf 2006: 99-100). Here, the strong use of 'no', reinforced through the pause marked by the insertion of two commas, demonstrates how categorical and determined Mrs. Ramsay is to resist her husband's stifling demands. By so doing, she shows that she is not a submissive wife who has internalized the traditional role. This idea is reinforced by her "flashing her needles, confident, upright" (Woolf 2006: 33). If she appears cold and distant towards her husband, her emotional aloofness is revealed to be a means for self-preservation. It is a way to protect herself from patriarchal oppression which is symbolically embodied through the pressure and demands of Mr. Ramsay and other male characters, such as Charles Tansley. Her resistance to Victorian rigidity is also expressed through her lack of severity in calling her daughters to order, for example, when Nancy laughs at her father's excessive reaction to Carmichael's request to be served "another plate of soup" (Woolf 2006: 78) which is a breach of Victorian table manners, or when Cam "stamped", "clenched her fist" (Woolf 2006: 21), and refuses to give William Bankes a flower as he asked for. Nancy's gentle mockery at her father's anger shows that she does not value the Victorian etiquette as much as he does, then Cam's refusal to give the flower, a symbol of femininity and emotional sensibility, to William Bankes underlines her rejection of the patriarchal figure's authority that Bankes stands for. Mrs. Ramsay's leniency towards her daughters' small liberty encourages her children's defiance of Victorian traditions. Christina Froula confirms that Mrs. Ramsay herself "secretly harbors infidel doubts, hoping in an unguarded moment that her daughters will "find a way out of it all" – some "simpler", "less laborious way" (Froula 2005: 138). Therefore, it signals that a part of this mother rejects the repressive principles of the time. Her distrust in the Victorian code of behaviour leads her, perhaps unintentionally, to stimulate her daughters' bold attitude, to "sport with infidel ideas which they had brewed for themselves of a life different from hers; in Paris perhaps; a wilder life; not always taking care of some man or other" (Woolf 2006: 9). Even though she is not a fully emancipated woman, Mrs. Ramsay's narcissism is a means to revolt against the unselfish characteristics women in their role, both as wife and mother, should possess, according to Victorian ideals. She is revealed to be quite the opposite of the self-effacing woman that society would like her to be. Additionally, as the main protagonist, her strong presence in the novel illustrates how "very influential" she is, "even after her death" (Daiches 1970: 67). She is the orbit around which the other characters revolved and "her personality dominates the book: she lives, in section three, in the memory of others; the character has become part of history, including and determining the present" (ibd.). Consequently, contrarily to Allison Pease who claims that "Woolf had to 'kill' Mrs. Ramsay, its outmoded 'angel,' but it was a necessary death" (Pease 2015: 90), this mother's spectral appearance at the end of the novel symbolically embodies the expression of the past returning to shape the present. Her come-back in Lily Briscoe's picture, through the line drawn in the centre, establishes that different personalities can meet in the middle. This intrusion of the past in the present is part of Woolf's refusal to construe that women necessarily have to fully reject the past traditions and conventions in order to escape from social oppression. This idea is supported by Suzanne Raitt who confirms that "Woolf appears to feel nostalgic for, as well as critical of, the ideal of Victorian womanhood" (Raitt 1990: 57). Mrs. Ramsay has not entirely succeeded in completely freeing herself from the ideal of Victorian womanhood, but her internal conflict proves that she is ready to negotiate her role within the system. She does not exactly match the definition of 'New Woman', but she certainly shows signs of rebellion, principally when she confesses that she can be herself when she is alone, namely when she is not performing her role of perfect hostess, mother or wife. This idea is emphasized in the following observation: "all the being and the doing, expansive, glittering, vocal, evaporated; and one shrunk, with a sense of solemnity, to being oneself, a wedge-shaped core of darkness" (Woolf 2006: 52). While Lily, on the one hand, epitomizes the Woolfian ideal of 'New Woman', as she privileges her artistic career over marriage and family, and thinks of her work as "a peaceful and exciting retreat" (Raitt 1990: 84), on the other hand, she also expresses mixed feelings, for example when she thinks that love "is also beautiful and necessary" (Woolf 2006: 84). Again, Woolf's nostalgia for the past is suggested through Lily's dilemma "to feel violently two opposite things at the same time" (Woolf 2006: 83). If this mechanism is revealed to act as a shield against patriarchal oppression exercised on women, Woolf also points out the ravages of another type of narcissism when she emphasizes the role it plays in the dehumanization prevailing during wartime.

5.3.2 The Havoc of Narcissism

The narrative technique that Woolf uses to report the death of the members of the Ramsay family is extremely compelling. Both Prue and Mrs. Ramsay's death are reported between brackets, very briefly, as if they were inconsequential. In fact, this is a way for Woolf to shock the reader. This ill-feeling is accentuated when Andrew Ramsay's death is related as follows: "[A shell exploded. Twenty or thirty young men were blown up in France, among them Andrew Ramsay, whose death, mercifully, was instantaneous]" (Woolf 2006: 109). The violence of the war is mirrored through words such as "exploded" and "blown up" which stress the brutality and damage of the war, while the narration persists in adopting a light and detached tone to report the tragic loss of one among many other men. Therefore, it de-dramatizes the death of these soldiers and simultaneously, it increases "the painfulness of these deaths by presenting them as insignificant within the larger picture" (Bazin/Lauter 1992: 21). It represents death as almost "unimportant only to the extent that the individual life is unimportant" (ibd.). Here, Woolf's criticism of war is expressed through her lament for those who have been lost. Through the trope of dead bodies and the Ramsay's decaying and deserted house as they are described in the chapter *Time Passes*, Woolf denounces the horrors of the Great War. Janet Winston confirms that this second section of the novel "represents the decade leading up to and including World War I as a period in which "no light of reason ruled the universe" (Bazin/ Lauter 1992: 67). Indeed, characterized as lifeless and wrecked by time, the Ramsay's house which was once very lively functions as a microcosm. It displays the ravages caused by the Great War through the comparison between the house and the battlefield: "the autumn trees, ravaged as they are, take on the flash of tattered flags kindling in the gloom of cool cathedral caves where gold letters on marble pages describe the death in battle and how bones bleach and burn far away in Indian sands" (Woolf 2006: 104-105). Through her narrative technique, the author denounces the little importance given to individuals during wartime. Roger Poole compares Woolf's use of brackets to "the new formalization and banalization of subjective reality that was introduced and made officially receivable by the Field Service Post Card" (Poole 1992: 84). He observes that "personal experience is reduced to a bare statement of fact, life and death are reduced to an item of news" (ibd.). Poole's analogy between the use of bracketed passages in *To the Lighthouse* and this official form denounces the dehumanization prevailing during wartime. It also reminds us of the detached and impersonal announcement of Mrs. Sinico's death in James Joyce's short story "A Painful Case". Poole notes that "with the telegraphic and telephonic communication of the First World War, this humanism has been obliterated. Now journalism in the modern sense has taken power. Now there were only "facts" – objectivity was triumphant" (Poole 1992: 85). In *Time Passes*, Woolf establishes a close connection between this idea of dehumanization and narcissism. The description of the empty house is accompanied with an allusion to Narcissus' death through the references to the "looking-glass", which "had once held a face" and the "flower reflected in water; its clear image on the wall opposite" (Woolf 2006: 106). Through intertextual references to the myth of Narcissus and her description of the battlefield (with the lost "pair of shoes" and the "shooting cap"), she seeks to expose human vanity and the individualism that she holds accountable for the harm engendered by World War I. Suzanne Raitt confirms that "the senselessness of the war stains the mirror-like surface of the sea – representing the cruel narcissism of nationalism" (Raitt 1990: 98). This is embodied through Woolf's reference to "a purplish stain upon the bland surface of the sea as if something has boiled and bled, invisibly, beneath" (Woolf 2006: 109). Andrew's death echoes the one of many other sons, who risked and lost their life "aimlessly", "in idiot games" (Woolf 2006: 110). With words such as "confusion", "wanton lust" and "amorphous" (ibd.), Woolf denounces the madness and the violence of the war and warns of the danger of disproportionate ego. Her criticism is analogous to Jean Rhys' denunciation of the rise of fascism in Europe, which led to the Second World War.

In her essay *A Room of One's Own*, Virginia Woolf declares that "women have served all these centuries as looking-glasses possessing the magic and delicious power of reflecting the figure of man at twice its natural" (Woolf 1949: 53). She adds that "without that power probably the earth would still be swamp and jungle" (ibd.). These words find their meaning in *To the Lighthouse*, which is female-centered and which allows Woolf to develop her social criticism. Through her depiction of the narcissistic mother, she shows that a self-absorbed parent is still capable of loving and caring for her children. Mrs. Ramsay is the perfect illustration of an affectionate and narcissistic mother who is blinded by the values she had internalized. The novel's treatment of the question of narcissism entails two levels of interpretation. First, the novel offers a sympathetic view of narcissistic mothers and thereby, challenges the prevailing biases on the issue. Woolf's exploration of narcissism constitutes a sharp criticism of Victorian values and is a means to undermine the idealized image of 'Angel in the House'. The female characters in *To the Lighthouse* attempt to protect themselves from male aggression and the pressure exercised by Victorian society through self-love. These narcissistic women are those who struggle for their emancipation. As part of their 'divided self', they have to face a major dilemma, namely the difficulty to break away from the past in order to embrace a new future. For Woolf, women need to negotiate their place within the system as there is no radical solution. Finally, the novel also explores the issue of narcissism in the light of violence occasioned by the Great War. It demonstrates that when narcissism is equivalent to an excessive, disproportionate ego, the outcome can be disastrous and that it can lead to the individual's objectification and dehumanization. Woolf, like Joyce in "A Painful Case" and Jean Rhys in *Good Morning, Midnight* distinguishes the two different types of narcissism that Freud has pointed out in his psychoanalytic work. In fact, Woolf's association of narcissism with nationalism in the context of the Great War parallels Jean Rhys' criticism of the rise of nationalism in Europe. While Woolf holds national pride accountable for the violence of the war, Rhys makes explicit that an individual's narcissistic self can also serve as a shield against fascism. Both Virginia Woolf and Jean Rhys offer an examination of narcissism from a psychological and socio-political angle and challenge this notion as personal diagnosis, instead they show that it has considerable explanatory power on a collective level.

6 "I'm a Cérébrale": A Mother's Isolation and Marginalization in Jean Rhys' *Good Morning, Midnight*

Sasha Jansen's bleak observation that "the street outside is narrow, cobbled-stoned, going sharply uphill and ending in a flight of steps. What they call an impasse" (Rhys 2000: 9) constitutes a metaphor of life as it is experienced by the heroine, namely a life full of obstacles, a deadlock and this image sets the tone of the novel. Following the disturbed mind of Sasha, a narcissistic mother, Jean Rhys invites her reader to dive into a world where appearances, prestige, and money have become the bedrock of society, in which youth and beauty are revealed to serve as female weapons but at the same time paradoxically as a curse. All these women strive to find their place in an environment, which demands of them to take an active part in mass consumption. Abounding with apparently contradictory elements, as the title of the novel immediately suggests, *Good Morning, Midnight* offers a criticism of interwar society as seen through the eyes of the female "flâneur", to use Charles Baudelaire's coinage which was popularized by Walter Benjamin. It also raises the problematic concept of female identity by addressing the taboos on sexuality and challenging the Victorian ideals of marriage and motherhood. Through the portrayal of Sasha Jansen, the writer explores the meanders of her heroine's narcissistic journey, from the quest to compensate for her sense of injury to her developing a positive image of self, and finally to make use of it, as a weapon to resist the rise of nationalism. It is within this scope that this chapter examines the novel's shift from individual psychology to socio-political criticism of the time.

6.1 SASHA'S NARCISSISTIC INJURY

The novel takes Sophia Jansen, alias Sasha, from London back to Paris where she once lived and underwent a series of humiliations and traumatic incidents, from the failure of her marriage to the death of her newborn son. Sasha recalls being "saved, rescued, fished-up, half-drowned, out of the deep, dark river, dry clothes, hair shampooed and set" (Rhys 2000: 10). As she wanders the city of Paris that she once knew well, Sasha is reminded of her painful past and haunted by the memory of her infant's death. Even if the episode of her infant's death is only briefly evoked, hence giving the impression that it is only a minor aspect, this incident is nevertheless key to the understanding of the novel. It is a decisive element in the description of the narcissistic mother that Sasha embodies. Although Rhys chooses to succinctly tell this episode, she nonetheless provides essential details of the before and after birth process Sasha goes through, making it one of the most vivid memories of her heroine and probably also the most vibrant moment of her narrative. First, when she arrives to give birth, Sasha remembers the place as being "a funny house", where "there are people having babies all over the place" (Rhys 2000: 49), but "no doctor to give chloroform here" because "this place is a place for poor people" (Rhys 2000: 50). She tells about the physical pain she experiences during labour and her psychological torture after giving birth. She worries about money and thinks that "they would crush him [her son] because we have no money – that is torture" (ibd.). Here, Sasha's financial concern is bound with the urgency to care for another human being, hence implying that the act of giving birth triggers her sense of responsibility for another individual than herself. Overwhelmed by anxiety and exhaustion, her thoughts become more and more agitated. She rambles on about money, the silence of the baby but in the midst of all this confusion, she discloses her strong connection to her newborn: "(This is not *a* child; this is *my* child [...])" (Rhys 2000: 50). Here, the bond between mother and son is established through the shift in the use of the italicized article, from "*a* child" to the possessive in "*my* child". Then, as she recognizes the child as being hers, she acknowledges with narcissistic satisfaction that he is in fact "a beautiful, beautiful baby" (Rhys 2000: 51). Angst-ridden, she constantly questions her ability to provide for the infant and also notices that something is at odds with him. The narration jumps from a brief reference to the child's stillness on the day of birth to the next day, when the nurse comes in and tells her patient: "'Now I am going to arrange that you will be just like what you were before. There will be no trace, no mark, nothing'" (ibd.). She swathes Sasha "up in very tight, very uncomfortable bandages. Intricately she rolls them and ties them" (ibd.). Both mother and son are described in similar terms: "And there I lie in these damned bandages for a week. And there he lies, swathed up too, like a little mummy. And never crying" (ibd.). Here, the text emphasizes the physical resemblance between mother and son. They are both wrapped up, thereby indicating Sasha's possible narcissistic connection to her child, who appears to be an extension of her own self. This idea is reinforced when she inspects her baby admiringly and concludes with satisfaction that his "eyebrows are drawn very faintly in gold dust" and that "his forehead is lovely" (ibd.). At the same time, this description through the analogy to a "little mummy" (Rhys 2000: 51) foreshadows the infant's death. This idea is reinforced by his unusual silence. Indeed, five weeks later Sasha contemplates her body "with not one line, not one wrinkle, not one crease" (Rhys 2000: 52). Then comparing her body with her infant's, she thinks: "there he is, lying with a ticket, tied round his wrist because he died in a hospital. And there I am looking down at him, without one line, without one wrinkle, without one crease" (ibd.). The repetition of the phrase "without one line, without one wrinkle, without one crease" on the one hand applies to Sasha's recovery. On the other hand, the structure of the sentence suggests that her son, who was also "swathed" in bandages, is also the one lying "without one line, without one wrinkle, without one crease". The aftermath of childbirth certainly contributes to Sasha's traumatic and painful memories, but her pregnancy which is described in more pleasurable terms reveals her happiness at the thought of becoming a mother: "my face is pretty, my stomach huge. [...] People are very kind to me. They get up and give me their seats in buses. Passe, Femme Sacrée. ... Not exactly like that, but still – it seemed to me that they were kind" (Rhys 2000: 110). Sasha's recollection of her pregnancy is written in present tense and accounts for the vivid and stimulating images she could never possibly forget. She experiences the joy of becoming mother as timeless and permanent. She confesses that: "the mound of my stomach is hidden under the bedclothes. So calm I feel, watching myself in the glass opposite [...] I am very well and very happy. I never think of what it will be like to have this baby or, if I think, it's as if a door shuts in my head" (Rhys 2000: 114). This is one of the rare scenes in the novel where Sasha displays signs of unconditional happiness, where the material does not matter any longer as the following words show: "I hardly ever think about money either". She feels "calm" and "very happy" and experiences a moment of pure maternal bliss, which makes it even harder to cope with her child's death. Wandering through the streets of Paris, Sasha is constantly brooding over her loss. Her "heart is heavy as lead, heavy as a stone" as she dwells on the memory that "he has a ticket tied around his wrist because he died. Lying so cold and still with a ticket round his wrist because he died" (Rhys 2000: 116). Here, the use of two very similar phrases, again both in content and structure emphasizes Sasha's inability to mourn the death of her son and put the past behind her. Seeking someone to blame for her misfortune, she concludes: "God is very cruel [...] very cruel. A devil, of course. That accounts for everything – the only possible explanation" (ibd.), she feels victimized. This tragedy marks the beginning of the heroine's plunge into darkness. She comments that "now the lights are red, dusky, haggard red, cruel red. Strings plucked softly by a man with a long thin nose and sharp, blue eyes. Our luck has changed and the lights are red." (Rhys 2000: 117). Red is an obvious reference to blood, the blood she shed while giving birth, and simultaneously a reminder of the death of her own flesh and blood. Reifying death under the appearance of a puppeteer who "plucked softly" the "strings" (ibd.) behind the scene, she is convinced that her fate has changed and concludes "only, it was after that that I began to go to pieces. Not all at once, of course. First this happened, and then that happened..." (Rhys 2000: 119).

And to her profound wound occasioned by her motherly grief comes a sequence of unfortunate events which further threatened her narcissistic self-esteem. One of them is the failure of her marriage to Enno, a *chansonnier* and journalist she met in London. He brought her to Paris promising her they would have a good life there. Then everything went very fast. She has not expected their relationship to take a serious turn, and the next thing she knew: "I wake up and it's my wedding-day, cold and rainy. [...] We get a taxi and drive through the rain to the town-hall and we are married with a lot of other couples, all standing round in a circle" (Rhys 2000: 96-97). Not only did Sasha and Enno get married on the spur of the moment, but then immediately after the ceremony, Enno displays signs of regret: "How idiotic all that business was!" (Rhys 2000: 97). Sasha begs her husband: "You won't ever leave me, will you?", to which he answers: "Allons, allons, a little gaiety" (ibd.), but their union is bound to fail. Later on, Enno verbally abuses and denigrates his pregnant wife. He reproaches her: "You don't know how to make love [...] you're too passive, you're lazy, you bore me. I've had enough of this. Goodbye" (Rhys 2000: 107). But it is only after their son's death that Enno leaves Sasha for good, even though he promises "I'll write", "I'll try to send you some money" (Rhys 2000: 118) before getting on the train. That the loss of their child could have been the initiator of their separation is conceivable even if it is not clearly stated in the text. However, what is certain is that Sasha has undergone a series of humiliations conducted by ruthless men such as Enno and Mr. Blank, the head of the department store where she used to work. All these undoubtedly contributed to aggravating her lack of self-esteem and in precipitating her urge to look for reparative measures. Furthermore, the incident at the department store is another illustration of Sasha's loss of self-esteem. When Mr. Blank asks her to take a letter to the register, which he mispronounces as the 'kise' instead of 'caisse', Sasha is unable to understand his instruction, and therefore, does not find the register. After wandering in the maze-like department store, she comes back to Mr. Blank's office with the letter. Then, after admitting that she could not find the 'kise', she becomes an easy prey for her boss' sarcastic remarks: "'Extraordinary,' he says, very slowly, 'quite extraordinary. God knows I'm used to fools, but this complete imbecility. ... This woman is the biggest fool I've ever met in my life. She seems to be half-witted. She's hopeless" (Rhys 2000: 24). Mr. Blank's use of the third person to refer to Sasha in her presence and his insults underline his abusive personality, as well as his lack of consideration for his employee. His arrogance is further stressed by his unwillingness to even bother learning the name of his staff: "Be as quick as you can, Mrs – er – please" (Rhys 2000: 22). Sasha is only one of the many pawns surrounding him. But if in this scene, Sasha is the one who is humiliated, ironically it is Mr. Blank, who is ridiculed. Earlier, he was assessing Sasha's language skills, especially her French knowledge, but in fact he is the one who has troubles with his French pronunciation. He turns out to expect from his employees a competence that he himself does not possess. This is indicated when he reproachfully tells Sasha: "I was told that the receptionist spoke French and German fluently" (Rhys 2000: 18).

Finally, the protagonist's mistreatment and narcissistic personality are best reflected through the description of the abused kitten, which acts as her double:

> The kitten had an inferiority complex and persecution mania and nostalgie de la boue and all the rest. You could see it in her eyes, her terrible eyes, that knew her fate. She was very thin, scraggy and hunted, with those eyes that knew her fate. Well, all the male cats in the neighbourhood were on to her like one o'clock. She

got a sore on her neck, and the sore on her neck got worse. 'Disgusting,' said the German hairdresser's English wife. 'She ought to be put away, that cat.' [...] 'She got run over. Mrs Greiner was going to take her to the chemist's to be put away, and she ran right out into the street.' Right out into the street she shot and a merciful taxi went over her. ... (Rhys 2000: 47)

The first resemblance between the kitten and Sasha is a physical one. After her wedding, Sasha looks at herself in the mirror and notices: "I look thin, – too thin – and dirty and haggard, with that expression that you get in your eyes when you are very tired..." (Rhys 2000: 102). Here, Sasha is described in similar terms as the "thin and "scraggy" kitten. Both of them are female, as the pronoun 'she' used to refer to the animal shows. Then, the cat is persecuted by its owners, just like Sasha is also victim of her employer's abuses. The kitten also suffers from a feeling of inferiority, which Sasha shows sign of, for instance, when she starts questioning her own qualifications and ability to work at the store, and believes that she was hired by pulling some strings: "I'm here because I have a friend who knows Mr Salvatini's mistress, and Mr Salvatini's mistress spoke to Mr Salvatini about me, and the day that he saw me I wasn't looking too bad and he was in a good mood" (Rhys 2000: 18). Both of them are surrounded by male characters who hurt them and leave them with scars, either physical or emotional ones. Furthermore, the kitten's death, which can be read as a form of suicide, echoes Sasha's own attempt to drown herself in the Seine or/and to drink herself to death. This analogy is later confirmed by the heroine when she declares: "in the glass just now my eyes were like that kitten's eyes. I sit without moving, unhappy" (Rhys 2000: 48).

If there is one cue that could possibly best describe Sasha's relationship to her appearance, that would be the famous phrase from 'Snow White' fairy tale: "mirror, mirror on the wall who is the fairest of all?". Like Mrs. Kearney and Mrs. Mooney in James Joyce's *Dubliners*, Sasha is constantly surrounded by reflective objects of all kind, the most obvious being the looking-glass. But instead of being a mere element of the setting, mirrors in *Good Morning, Midnight,* are permanently present in the protagonist's daily life. The looking-glass' reflecting surface assists Sasha in her narcissistic assessment of her appearance. It also allows her to define and judge the places she visits, such as restaurants, bars and hotel rooms. One of the rooms she occupied is described as having "nothing in it but a bed and a looking-glass" (Rhys 2000: 83), as if along with the bed, the presence of a mirror was enough to make a room a liveable area. Mirrors define a place and also play the role of an intimate companion. Always carrying one in her bag (see Rhys 2000: 47), the looking-glass fulfils Sasha's self-obsessive need to check her appearance when it pleases her, hence it validates her self-gratification.

6.2 ON THE LOOKOUT FOR REPARATIVE MEASURES

Within the frame of the protagonist's self-infatuation with her physical appearance, her excessive obsession with fashion commodities is emphasized. It becomes a means to sooth her narcissistic scar. Originally her move to Paris was encouraged by her friend Sidonie who saw Sasha's relocation as a chance for her to escape her depression and grief. Convincing her friend of the positive effects this move represents, she tells her: "I think you need a change. Why don't you go back to Paris for a bit?...You could get yourself some new clothes – you certainly need them... I'll lend you the money" (Rhys 2000: 11). Sidonie's argument shows that clothes are believed to possess the ability to improve one's destiny. A connection between garment and happiness is established throughout the novel. Almost after every dark, humiliating, and sad episode an allusion to clothing is made, as if clothes have a cathartic effect on the character. For instance, after being humiliated by Mr. Blank, and after losing her job at the prestigious dresshouse, Sasha, who dissolves in tears, seeks refuge in one of the fitting-rooms, and at the thought of the little black dress she fancies, suddenly stops crying:

> I cry for a long time [...] in this fitting-room there is a dress in one of the cupboards which has been worn a lot by the mannequins and is going to be sold off for four hundred francs. The saleswoman has promised to keep it for me. I have tried it on; I have seen myself in it. It is a black dress with wide sleeves embroidered in vivid colours – red, green, blue, purple. It is my dress. If I had been wearing it I should never have stammered or been stupid. (Rhys 2000: 25)

This scene shows that the dress has the ability to empower women by increasing their self-confidence ("If I had been wearing it I should never have stammered or been stupid"). It discloses Sasha's belief in the important role appearance plays in determining one's fate. This is visible in other scenes, for instance when at Théodore's restaurant, Sasha experiences a strong feeling of discomfort: "my throat shuts up, my eyes sting. This is awful. Now I am going to cry. This is worst...If I do I shall really have to walk under a bus when I get outside" (Rhys 2000: 44). Again, she shies away from her uneasiness by concentrating her thoughts on her physical appearance: "I try to decide what colour I shall have my hair dyed, and hang on that thought as you hang on to something when you are drowning. Shall I have it red? Shall I have it black? Now, black – that would be starting. Shall I have it blond cendré?" (ibd.). In this passage, there is no clear-cut transition from Sasha's expression of distress to her obsession with her hair. This indicates how her absorption in her physical appearance functions as a distraction from her feeling of shame and humiliation to the point of relieving her, at least temporarily, from uncomfortable situations. Besides the apparent comfort fashion seems to provide to Rhys' heroine, passages referring to dresses, hats, coats, and hair occupy an important part of the narrative and they seem to follow Sasha on her search for happiness and personal fulfilment. More than simply having a cathartic effect on the character, this strong desire to change one's appearance addresses the issue of unstable identity, which emphasizes Sasha's difficulty in finding her place in society. She oscillates between her desire to conform to the materialistic society and her own need to find her true self, even if it means to remain a social outcast. When she declares: "I must go and buy a hat this afternoon, I think, and tomorrow a dress. I must get on with the transformation act" (Rhys 2000: 53), the use of the modal 'must' suggests that on the one hand, Sasha has the urge to compensate for her loss of narcissistic supply through material goods, at the same time as she feels compelled by society to go through physical and emotional metamorphosis. Then, the word association "transformation" and "act" reinforces the idea that she needs to play the part of someone she is not really. And as much as physical appearance contributes to social acceptance, Rhys shows that it can also be deceitful, as proved by René who, misled by Sasha's fancy coat, approaches her, believing she looks like "a wealthy dame trotting round Montparnasse" (Rhys 2000: 61). Also, her narcissistic desire to keep up appearances goes hand in hand with her wish to remain forever young. Influenced by both her need for admiration and the culture of consumerism, Sasha tries to hide the stamps of time by "powder[ing] her face" (Rhys 2000: 101). While she desperately tries to look for reparative measures for her narcissistic injury through the use of cosmetics, Sasha reveals the other side of the coin, offering a more positive interpretation of narcissism. Rishona Zimring informs us that the arrival of cosmetics on the marketplace was understood as the embodiment of women's liberation, suggesting a clear break-up from Victorian ideologies, which demanded of women to remain natural and discreet at all time. In the act of powdering one's face in public, Zimring explains that "this means asserting one's freedom from domesticity and Victorian conventions of femininity that assign women to the natural, not the artificial" (Zimring 2000: 219). Referring to Kathy Peiss' *Hope in a Jar* (1998), Rishona Zimring insists that "in a general sense, cosmetics signified the transgressive femininity of the non-domestic woman; the made-up female face connoted abandonment of an idea, the nineteenth-century 'natural face' [...] that was supposed to convey fixity and essence of identity removed from fashion and consumption" (Zimring 2000: 219). However, this idea of freedom that the 'cosmetic mask' seems to convey, remains ambiguous, for as Zimring observes the 'mask' "defines femininity as appearance, and as such it associates femininity with the rise of an alienated individualism" (Zimring 2000: 220). Still within this vision of women's emancipation through the politics of consumerism, Rhys by setting her novel within the metropolis of Paris, at the time when massive department stores were blooming in big cities, shows how consumer culture in the interwar period redefines the urban landscape through consumption of mass-produced goods, encouraged by a general rise of the standard of living. These phenomena, Alissa Karl explains:

> once a predominantly upper – and middle – class activity, shopping as entertainment and pleasure also extends through the class spectrum in the interwar period, as the masses are invited to participate via the expansion of retail outlets (such as chain stores), and through the proliferation of cheaper mass-produced goods marketed to them. (Karl 2009: 17-18)

Along with the increase of women's buying power, Karl suggests, 'the now – iconographic short hair', 'short dresses', and 'boyish or the unisex fashion of the 1920s' also marked a turning point for women, because these changes in female appearance question the whole concept of gender identity, at a time when in both British and French society "women were negotiating their femininity and their 'emancipation' – how they lived, what they wore, and what demands they made of male-run political establishments – simultaneously at the level of politics and fashion" (Karl 2009: 18). Karl also clarifies that "even the woman who didn't transform herself into a 'modern girl' by shortening her skirt or cutting her hair was still integrated into the mass marketplace on a daily basis as she ran the household or shopped for personal items" (ibd.). Yet, Rachel Bowlby discloses the other face of consumerism when she writes that "while woman is simultaneously aided in and 'emancipated' from her domestic tasks by household gadgets, the making of women into avid consumers fits comfortably into a story of male seduction of women where women are understood as compliant with the men who dictate their desire to them" (Bowlby 1985: 19-20). Reflecting upon the economic conditions of consumerism, Sasha observes:

> All that is left in the world is an enormous machine, made of white steel. It has innumerable flexible arms, made of steel. Long, thin arms. At the end of each arm is an eye, the eyelashes stiff with mascara. When I look more closely I see that only some of the arms have these eyes – others have lights. The arms that carry the eyes and the arms that carry the lights are all extraordinarily flexible and very beautiful. But the grey sky, which is the background, terrifies me... And the arms wave to an accompaniment of music and of song. Like this: 'Hotcha – hotcha – hotcha...' And I know the music; I can sing the song... (Rhys 2000: 156-157)

This scene is central to the depiction of Rhys' heroine. Sasha describes consumer society as an "enormous machine", with "innumerable flexible arms, made of steel". Thereby, she reveals her awareness of the double-bind of consumerism. When she declares "I know the music; I can sing the song", it implies that her knowledge of consumer practices enables her to foil the traps of consumerism and is an overt statement of her refusal to remain a passive victim on the marketplace. Sasha willingly chooses to put on the fashion mask and to perform, hence allowing herself to shine for a moment, to become the object of the male gaze, and thereby, satisfy her narcissistic urges. Kirsten Fest observes "there is a distinct theatricality to the scene. The background is meticulously described, it appears almost like a carefully designed stage or film set" (Fest 2009: 205). In Sasha's case, clothes are employed as costume, the urban landscape of Paris functions as a stage and the male

A Mother's Isolation and Marginalization | 145

gaze becomes source of narcissistic gratification. Finally, being a woman in Modernist consumer society means performing and masquerading femininity. Clothes as well as make-up become props, which help Sasha in fulfilling her theatrical role. Additionally, the way Sasha interacts with men, Kerstin Fest notes "is clearly not meant to be a depiction of 'natural' courting behaviour but is rather like a complex and well-rehearsed dance" (Fest 2009: 90). Although Jean Rhys suggests that fashion and consumer culture act as reparative measures for Sasha's narcissistic self, she also indicates that they reinforce women's sense of need. With the development of marketing strategy and the use of new tricks, such as the setting up of department stores, Rhys shows how these help in creating and maintaining the desire of the female shopper. The large shop windows, presenting alluring products, young mannequins or the dummies with an ideal figure, displaying in an attractive way the latest fashion collection, certainly aim at seducing women, so as to incite them to purchase and covet fashion commodities. Sasha clearly shows envy at the sight of the dummies and confesses: "I would feel as if I were drugged, sitting there, watching those damned dolls, thinking what a success they would have made of their lives if they had been women. Satin skin, silk hair, velvet eyes, sawdust heart – all complete" (Rhys 2000: 16). As she contemplates the dolls, Sasha feels like being under the influence of narcotics, alluding once again to her material addiction and her obsession with physical appearance, which reflects her narcissistic projection on the dolls. Admiring the power of seduction that these dolls possess, Sasha wishes she could be one of them. She sees in them this ideal self she longs for and illustrates Karl's statement that "consumer culture transforms the narcissistic mirror into a shop window, the glass which reflects an idealized image of the woman who stands before it, in the form of the model she could buy or become" (Karl 2009: 26). Consumer culture reinforces the narcissistic needs of women, who are convinced that a well-groomed appearance will bring them a step closer to this illusion of an ideal self, an impression sustained by the shop windows and consumerism. Moreover, this illusion is further suggested by the fake atmosphere of the department store where Sasha used to work. Alissa Karl notes that "the setting for this scene, a clothing shop, has been decorated with its own symbolic of false objects" (Karl 2009: 43). The setting of the store is described as "a large white – and – gold room with a dark-polished floor. Imitation Louis Quinze chairs, painted screens, three or four elongated dolls, beautifully dressed, with charming and malicious faces" (Rhys 2000: 16). In the previous description, the use of the words "imitation" and "painted" underlines the prioritization of the fake over the genuine, while Sasha's reference to the "charming and malicious oval faces", functions as synecdoche which discloses the alluring but deceiving features of department stores. It also shows that Sasha is well aware of the machinations of the marketplace. This claim is confirmed when Sasha states: "you can almost see the strings that are pulling the puppets" (Rhys 2000: 75). Through this statement, she confirms that she can no longer be fooled. Finally, Sasha can no longer be seen as passive victim. As a result, we can conclude that Rhys proposes that Sasha's self-absorption should be contemplated under a more positive light.

6.3 THE NEW FACE OF THE 'FLÂNEUR'

To the depiction of a self-absorbed mother who tries at all costs to compensate for her narcissistic injury through the acquisition of fashion commodities, Rhys also suggests that Sasha is still capable of showing empathy and generosity, especially towards social outcasts. For example, she recalls encountering an old Englishwoman and her daughter when she was working as sale assistant and expresses her disapproval for the way the bald woman is reprimanded by her daughter, who feels ashamed of her mother's bald skull and her desire to buy a hat to hide it. Sasha remembers the daughter bursting out with anger: "Well, you made a perfect fool of yourself, as usual. You've had everybody in the shop sniggering. If you want to do this again, you'll have to do it by yourself. I refuse, I refuse" (Rhys 2000: 20). As she remembers the old lady's face, "her eyes still undaunted but something about her mouth and chin collapsing" (ibd.), Sasha assumes the role of defender of the weak and thinks: "oh, but why not buy her a wig, several decent dresses, as much champagne as she can drink, all the things she likes to eat and oughtn't to, a gigolo if she wants one?" (ibd.). Sasha adopts a very liberal stance, which reveals her open-mindedness and also her desire for independence. The lifestyle she is promoting is one that she has ended up adopting, and which proves to, at least temporarily, alleviate her pain. Furthermore, other instances in the novel point at Sasha's ability to show compassion. Even if money seems to occupy her thoughts, she still proves to be charitable towards more needy people. One morning as Sasha was leaving her hotel, she encounters a little old woman who asks her for money. Without hesitation, Sasha "give[s] her two francs" (Rhys 2000: 42). She recalls: "as I go past the baker's shop at the corner of the street she comes out, with a long loaf of bread, smiles at me and waves gaily, I wave back. For a moment I escape from myself" (ibd.). This brief episode, which comes unpredicted and has no clear connection with the previous or the next scene in the narration, reinforces the idea that Sasha's generosity is a spontaneous and unconditional act. She finds satisfaction at the sight of the joy that the "loaf of bread" gives to the old woman. Finally, it seems that this slant of generosity brings out the best in the heroine, who confirms that "for a moment I escape from myself". Later, Sasha also demonstrates sign of empathy for her Russian friend Delmar, to whom she feels apologetic for requesting that they take a taxi to go to the painter's place: "when I see how anxiously he is watching the meter I am sorry I insisted on taking a taxi. All the same, I should have dropped dead if I had tried to walk this distance" (Rhys 2000: 71). Therefore, considerate to her friend, she offers: "Do let me pay, because it was I who insisted" (ibd.). And once back to her room and even after she realized that he had the money to pay for the taxi fare: "I start worrying about him and the money he has to spend on me" (Rhys 2000: 86). Sasha is certainly a narcissist, who shows compassion for marginalized others, with whom she empathizes for knowing only too well herself how it feels to be a social outcast. And when she purchases one of Serge's paintings, which represents "an old Jew with a red nose, playing the banjo" (Rhys 2000: 83), Sasha again renews her act of generosity by supporting the artist. While on the one hand, her acquisition of the over-priced painting can be read as a scam, on the other hand it can be interpreted as a kind of philanthropic engagement. When Serge tells Sasha: "'I'll tell you what you can do for me – you can find some other idiots who'll buy my pictures'" (Rhys 2000: 84), the word "idiot" can be read as an insult. However, when it is combined with terms such as "smiles", "gently" and "disarmingly" as in "when he says this, he smiles at me so gently, so disarmingly. The touch of the human hand. ... I'd forgotten what it was like, the touch of the human hand" (ibd.), the use of apparently derogatory terms is nuanced and can even be seen as affective. This is stressed by Sasha's allusion to the "touch of the human hand", which insists on Serge's sympathy for the heroine and is confirmed when seeing her off, "he gives my hand a long, hard shake and says 'Amis'" (ibd.). Sasha remembers this episode as a very happy moment, which extirpates her feeling of melancholia and sadness. She confesses that "Now I am not thinking of the past at all. I am well in the present" (ibd.). Sasha gives the impression of constantly being between two stools, namely her past and her present. She shows signs of unhappiness and depression mainly whenever she thinks of her past. However, when she chooses to adopt the *'carpe diem'* doctrine to seize the day and enjoy the moment, she displays a totally new self. She exhibits a more independent and ecstatic self, when she incarnates the figure of "prototypical window-shopping flaneur" (Dell' Amico 2005: 16). On many occasions, Sasha claims her independence, for example, at the beginning of the novel, when she tells that: "I have been here five days. I have decided on a place to eat in at midday, a place to eat at night, a place to have my drink in after dinner. I have arranged my little life" (Rhys 2000: 9). The repetitive use of the personal pronoun "I", combined with the verb "have", clearly states that Sasha is master of her own decisions. She actively takes control of her new life in Paris and chooses no longer to be a passive victim. This is reflected in her statement: "no more meals with the destitute girls" (Rhys 2000: 120). Instead, she settles for a routine, which consists in actively consuming products of all kinds, according to her motto to "Eat. Drink. March" (ibd.), and as Sasha announces: "just the sensation of spending, that's the point" (Rhys 2000: 121). By depicting an independent heroine, who violates the normative codes and the social expectations for women, Rhys demonstrates that Sasha can no longer be seen as a victim. Elaine Savory emphasizes that Sasha, who "is clear-sighted about her addiction breaks two social expectations: that women should not drink strong alcohol and that women should not drink alone" (Savory 2009: 70). But most importantly, she shows that through her drugs and alcohol consumption she finds a way to express the "repressed inner core of her emotional life" (ibd.) and feel liberated. Also, while formerly she has been suspected of trading her body for money, in her new life in Paris, the dynamic is reversed. Formerly, Sasha received money from men such as Mr. Lawson. Even if their sexual intercourse is not explicitly stated, what follows nevertheless suggests Sasha's guilt for trading her body. Questioned by Enno about the origin of the money, Sasha breaks out in tears declaring: "I want to have a bath. I want another dress. I want clean underclothes. I feel so awful. I feel so dirty" (Rhys 2000: 101). The reference to the dirty underwear and her urge to "have a bath" indicates Sasha's attempt to reclaim her purity. And now, the new Sasha is the one who picks up gigolos from the theatre for her own enjoyment (see Rhys 2000: 61). Strolling around Paris, actively consuming through the act of eating, drinking, purchasing and making love, Rhys' protagonist investigates the city in the same way that Walter Benjamin's 'flâneur' explores the streets of the metropolis. According to Benjamin, the flâneur's home is "the arcades, a rather recent invention of industrial luxury" (Benjamin 1985: 37). He describes the arcades as "glass-covered, marble-panelled passageways through the entire complexes of houses" (ibd.). They "are lighted from above, are lined with the most elegant shops, so that such an arcade is a city, even a world, in miniature" (ibd.). Benjamin concludes that "It is in this world that the *flâneur* is at home […] The street becomes a dwelling for the flâneur; he is as much at home among the façades of houses as a citizen is in his four walls" (ibd.). Here, a resemblance with Sasha's environment can be established. As mentioned before, the novel opens on a description of the city, immediately with a first glimpse on "the street outside" (see Rhys 2000: 9), before shifting to a minute depiction of the numerous department stores (see Rhys 2000: 16-25), and this observation is always conducted through the heroine's eyes. Sasha's intimacy with the city is emphasized through these detailed descriptions and as she wanders in the city, the reader's gaze follows her everywhere she goes. Benjamin explains that "interpersonal relationships in big cities are distinguished by a marked preponderance of the activity of the eye over the activity of the ear" (Benjamin 1985: 38). This is mainly due to the development of public means of transportation (buses, railroads and trams) in the nineteenth century which puts people in a "position of having to look at one another for long minutes or even hours without speaking to one another" (ibd.). If in *Good Morning, Midnight*, there are very few references to public transportation, with the exception of the London tube station and a reference to taxis, the gaze is nevertheless constantly emphasized, for instance in the department store, at the multiple bars, restaurants and coffee shops where Sasha hangs out, as well as the different hotels where she stays. These places allow personal interactions to take place and the mutual gaze exchange sustains and reinforces Sasha's narcissistic needs. Having the impression of continually being watched and judged, for instance at Théodore's restaurant (see Rhys 2000: 43), Sasha's obsession in keeping up appearances is reinforced. In this scene, the sight is stressed under all its different forms, from a quick ("watch" and "look") to a more insistent look ("stare" and "fixed"). Either paranoid or lucid, Sasha's observation that "everybody in the room is staring at her" and that "all the eyes in the room are fixed on her" (Rhys 2000: 43) underlines her needs to be the centre of attention. Finally, Sasha embodies the narcissistic 'flâneur', who "abandoned in the crowd", "shares the situation of the commodity" and surrenders to "the intoxication of the commodity around which surges the stream of customers"

(Benjamin 1985: 55). Sasha, who is often under the influence of substances (luminal and alcohol), and dependent on fashion commodities, matches Benjamin's observation on "the charm displayed by addicts under the influence of drugs" (Benjamin 1985: 56). He notes that "commodities derive the same effect from the crowd that surged around and intoxicates them. The concentration of customers which makes the markets, which in turn makes the commodity into a commodity, enhanced its attractiveness to the average buyer" (ibd.). Yet, since Sasha is aware of the stakes of consumerism, she can enjoy and investigate consumer society as an "unwilling detective" (Benjamin 1985: 40). In Rhys' novel, the narcissistic mother turns out to embody the new face of the 'flâneur'. Emily Stanback notes that "the roots of the peripatetic are philosophical – the name is derived from the appellation for Aristotle's disciples – and peripatetic walking is often portrayed as a means of moral growth, particularly, and problematical, through edifying encounters with the laboring poor" (Stanback 2013: 147) and it is precisely this image that Rhys' heroine reflects. Sasha's personal development is evident through the sharp contrast between the Sasha of before and the present Sasha who incarnates the image of independent 'flâneur'. The protagonist's before and after image is underlined in her memory of the department store. Sasha imagines how she could and should have confronted her employer as her internal monologue points out:

> Let's say that you have the mystical right to cut my legs off. But the right to ridicule me afterwards because I am a cripple – no, that I think you haven't got. And that's the right you hold most dearly, isn't it? You must be able to despise people you exploit. But I wish you a lot of trouble, Mr Blank, and just to start off with, your damned shop's going bust. (Rhys 2000: 26)

Sasha clearly expresses her wish to defy Mr. Blank, which only comes with hindsight, but is key in revealing her moral growth. At that point, she also demonstrates her ability to think critically, which is best summed up when outraged, she declares: "well, let's argue this out, Mr Blank. You, who represent Society, have the right to pay me four hundred francs a month. That's my market value, for I am an inefficient member of Society, slow in the uptake, uncertain, slightly damaged in the fray, there's no denying it" (Rhys 2000: 25). It becomes apparent that Sasha has learned from her experiences. She denounces the underhand practices of the political economy of her time and shows that she can no longer be fooled by the system. At that point, she is revealed to be an important figure of the metropolitan and consumer landscape, who acquires her expertise through her various personal experiences and encounters with outcasts. Turned into a social critic, the character of Sasha allows a more positive reading of the narcissistic mother. Although her obsession with her appearance is one of her main daily preoccupations, she is nonetheless the living proof that she can still be concerned with others, what according to René are the attributes of a "cérébrale": "'A cérébrale,' he says, seriously, 'is a woman who doesn't like men or need them.'" (Rhys 2000: 136). Then he further explains: "...but a cérébrale doesn't like women either. Oh, no. The true cérébrale is a woman who likes nothing and nobody except herself and her own damned brain or what she thinks is her brain'" (ibd.). The definition René provides, describes the "cérébrale" as both a narcissist and a thinker, and therefore to some extent implies Sasha's ability to reflect on the present socio-political situation of the time. Indeed, through the figure of the "flâneur", Rhys shows political concerns, since at that time Europe was witnessing the rise of fascism. In fact, allusions to the question of nationality abound in the novel. Sasha is constantly reminded that she is a foreigner and is repeatedly asked to prove her citizenship, for example when she moves in the new room, the tenant insists on seeing her passport because "Nationality – that's what has puzzled him. I ought to have put nationality by marriage" (Rhys 2000: 13). Sasha is aware that the patron judges her by her look, especially by her hat which draws attention to her status as an alien: "I tell him I will let him have the passport in the afternoon and he gives my hat a gloomy, disapproving look. I don't blame him. It shouts 'Anglaise' my hat" (ibd.). Here, the mistrust and suspicion that foreigners encounter are underlined, and it shows that even if Sasha speaks the language and has been living in Paris for a while, she nevertheless remains marginalized based on her passport. Sasha's *flânerie* in the streets of Paris, which creates opportunity for new encounters, further stresses the importance of one's national belonging in determining the position one occupied in society during the years between the two World Wars. Most of the acquaintances she made are expatriates. Serge Rubin and his friends are believed to be Russians, perhaps also Ukrainians, among whom one of them has been naturalized French. René, the gigolo, could be a French-Canadian who lived in Morocco for a while. However, his origins are obscured as Sasha's reaction stipulates: "I'll tell you one thing I don't believe. I don't believe you're French-Canadian" (Rhys 2000: 63). To her scepticism, René asks "Then what do you think I am?" (ibd.). She finally answers "Spanish? Spanish-American?" (ibd.). This exchange between Sasha and René insists once again on the importance of nationality at the time and the bias surrounding the discourse on national affiliation. The fact that René could be mistaken for a Canadian, a Spanish or a Spanish-American suggests what an abstract gauge and therefore how unreliable and frivolous it is to judge an individual according to their national identity. Then, the novel presents the gathering of foreigners as a sign of their marginalization from a society, which seeks to promote national identity through racial discrimination. Rhys warns of the consequences through the episode of the Martiniquaise, which is a blatant occurrence of racism against foreigners. The Martiniquaise, "half-negro – a mulatto" (Rhys 2000: 79) felt the hostilities of her neighbours because "she wasn't white" (Rhys 2000: 80). She reports that "every time they looked at her she could see how they hated her, and that the other people in the streets looked at her the same way" (ibd.). She recalls being insulted by the little girl of one of the tenants, who had told her that "she was a dirty woman, that she smelt bad, that she hadn't any right in the house" (Rhys 2000: 81). The antagonism and hatred she suffered have deeply transformed this woman, who "was like something that has turned into a stone" (Rhys 2000: 80). In this scene, the narration echoes the three main tropes of the grotesque: 'doubleness' and 'hybridity' which are embodied though the character of the 'mulatto' and the third trope 'metamorphosis' is suggested through the analogy between the woman and a stone. This idea is confirmed by Delmar's comment that he had the impression he "was talking to something that was no longer human, no longer quite alive" (ibd.). Rhys uses the grotesque to depict the general audience's reaction when facing alterity. On the one hand, it casts light on the cruelty and inhumanity of those who find pleasure in persecuting minorities; on the other hand, it aims at triggering compassion for the woman. Sasha shows empathy for the 'mulatto' when she admits that "it's a very sad story" (ibd.) and concludes that "most human beings have cruel eyes. That rosy, wooden, innocent cruelty" (Rhys 2000: 81). This remark is emphasized by Delmar's observation that the child in question was "only seven or eight, and yet she knew so exactly how to be cruel and who it was safe to be cruel to" (ibd.). He concludes by stating that for this, "one must admire Nature" (ibd.). This illustration of cruelty only confirms what Sasha has anticipated: "homo homini lupus" (Rhys 2000: 21) that is 'a man is a wolf to another man', which foreshadows the rise of fascism in Europe. Moreover, the novel starts and ends with a reference to the 'Exhibition', which, as Mary Lou Emery and other critics have suggested, is a direct allusion to the '1937 Exposition Internationale des Arts et des Techniques Appliqués à la Vie Moderne'. The goal of the 1937 Exhibition, which took place in Paris was to allow different countries such as France, Germany, the Soviet Union, Italy and Spain to compete in producing a neo-classical master piece which would embody the unity of the people. However, rather it turned out to express the exact opposite through massive constructions reflecting the nationalist pride and the grandiosity of the country. For instance, France, with its 55 Pavilions, each one representing a colony, appears to offer propaganda which shows off the domination and success of the country, while on the other hand, the German "neo-classical tower with its National-Socialist eagle perching atop a Swastika" (Herbert 1995: 96), was facing the enormous "Worker and Collective Farm Woman", representing the greatness of the Soviet Union, as well as its national pride. Ihor Junyk confirms that the '1937 Exposition Internationale' valued the promotion of national identity and propaganda. He explains that originally the fairs "provided a forum for the display and comparison of consumer goods" (Junyk 2013: 106). However, with the expansion of nationalist movements in Europe and their boundless attempt "to 'invent' national traditions, the expositions saw the increased popularity of discrete national pavilions, which began to displace the more fluid, cosmopolitan exhibition spaces by the early 1900s" (ibd.). Junyk notes that historians such as Shanny Peer and Eric Hobsbawn have agreed that by 1937 "the Exposition Internationale had become the ideal forum for the projection of a representation of the nation to the rest of the world" (Junyk 2013: 106). Therefore, the '1937 Exposition Internationale', where the national pavilions "were routinely anthropomorphized, discursively transforming them into avatars of the nation" discloses the narcissism of these countries. Michael Taussig names this attitude "state fetishism" (Taussig 1993: 218). This term describes the tendency to "casually identify 'the State' as being unto itself, animated with a will and mind of its own" (ibd.). This connection between national identity and narcissism finds its significance through Sigmund Freud's 'Narcissism of Minor Differences' (NMD) that he applies to both individual psychology and philosophy of culture. At the beginning, the term 'narcissism of minor differences' referred to "a special kind of morbid self-love that builds upon an exaggerated notion of how the person differs from the people around him/her" (Kolstø 2007: 156). Later, it was applied to relations among groups and suggested that "group members embrace their group with an excessive love because they see it as radically different from other groups" (ibd.). Freud used the term 'Narcissism of Minor Differences' in *Taboo of Virginity* (1917) for the first time, based on the anthropologist Ernest Crawley's thoughts and claimed that these are "the sources of feelings of strangeness and hostility" (Kolstø 2007: 157) between people. Then, later in *Group Psychology and the Analysis of the Ego* (1921), Freud develops his concept by applying it to the relationship between nations and between regional groups within nations. This brought him to the conclusion that "communities with adjoining territories, and related to each other as well, that are engaged in constant feuds and in ridiculing each other – like the Spaniards and the Portuguese, for instance, the North Germans and the South Germans, the English and the Scots and so on" (Kolstø 2007: 157). Finally, in *Civilization and its Discontents* (1930), Freud investigates the sociological function of NMD and concludes that "It is always possible to bind together a considerable number of people in love, so long as there are other people left over to receive the manifestations of their aggressiveness" (ibd.). He argues that it is through the aggression towards 'outsiders' that the tight relationship within the group is ensured. Since *Civilization and its Discontents* was written in 1930, three years before Hitler's access to power and eight years before Freud had to flee Germany, it is very likely that Freud's work was influenced by the socio-political upheaval of the time. If Rhys does not explicitly write about dictatorship and antisemitism, however, the marginalization of her heroine and the other social outcasts she encounters in the streets of the metropolis is reminiscent of the socio-psychological mechanism of 'Narcissism of Minor Differences'. She emphasizes the division between Caucasians and people of colour in the passage about the Martiniquaise's treatment. She isolates the woman from the "the people in the streets" and "everybody" (Rhys 2000: 80) else. The words "everybody" and "the people in the streets" refer to the crowd and implies their indoctrination through propaganda which dehumanizes and spreads hatred towards minorities. Rhys underlines the potential danger that the masses represent when they are unified and institutionalized. She approaches in a subtle way the issue of antisemitism through Sasha's observation of Serge: "this is late October, 1937 [...] the friend is a Jew of about forty. He has that mocking look of the Jew, the look that can be so hateful, that can be so attractive, that can be so sad" (Rhys 2000: 76). Noteworthy is the reference to the date, the only time indicator in the whole novel, which provides a context to Rhys' socio-political criticism. Then, the description of

Serge, which starts off with a cliché shows that Sasha is first wary of the painter. However, this is immediately nuanced by the adjectives "hateful", "attractive" and "sad", which imply that Serge has different facets, like everyone else, hence it denounces the absurdity of prejudices. Helen Carr observes that Serge, despite his "mocking look", does not try to sneer at Sasha but that "like Sasha, Serge is conscious of the prejudice about him, and angry at the cruelty that it inflicts" (Carr 1996: 62). In fact, he "starts getting hold of her" and "they find they share a love of 'negro music', which for Rhys represents the world of emotions [...] as opposed to the hard-boiled calculating world of the English" (ibd.). Both Sasha and Serge are unfairly recognized as alien and through their marginalization, they have eventually realized the political and social issues at stakes. Like, René who at the Exhibition "sees the Trocadero's Star of Peace" and "ominously denounces it as 'mesquin [...] vulgar [...] mesquin, your Star of Peace'" (Carr 1996: 74), Sasha also distressingly expresses her need to find the way out of the Exhibition:

> I am in the passage of a tube station in London. Many people are in front of me; many people are behind me. Everywhere there are placards printed in red letters. This Way to the Exhibition, This Way to the Exhibition. But I don't want the way to the Exhibition – I want the way out. There are passages to the right and passages to the left, but no exit sign. Everywhere the fingers point and the placards read: This Way to the Exhibition… I touch the shoulder of the man walking in front of me. I say: 'I want the way out'. But he points to the placards and his hand is made of steel. I walk along with my head bent, very ashamed, thinking: 'Just like me – always wanting to be different from other people.' The steel finger points along a long stone passage. This Way – This Way – This Way to the Exhibition. (Rhys 2000: 12)

Encircled and overwhelmed by the crowd, Sasha reiterates her desire of "wanting to be different from other people". Her assertion is an overt rejection of mass propaganda and stresses her wish to stand out of the indoctrinated crowd. Then, her refusal to go either 'left' or 'right' insists on her "rejection of both Soviet and fascist solutions to Europe's predicament" (Dell' Amico 2005: 28). Sasha chooses to remain a social outcast because it implies refusing to act as dictated by society. On many occasions, she reasserts her choice to subvert rather than reflect the reactionary program of nationalism. Caught in her frenzy of purchasing, Sasha acquires a painting representing "an old Jew with a red nose, playing the banjo" (Rhys 2000: 83), which quite realist in style, simultaneously suggests hybridity; and so do the other paintings which fascinate Sasha: "the misshapen dwarfs juggling with huge coloured balloons", "the four-breasted woman" or "the hopeless old prostitute wait[ing] outside the urinoir" (Rhys 2000: 84). Art was an important medium in propaganda, at the time and was extensively influenced by socio-political factors. In Picasso's work, for instance, "two styles unproblematically reflect the different values and dominant ideologies of pre-war and post-war Paris" (Junyk 2013: 5). Junyk explains that "cubist fragmentation is clearly associated with the cosmopolitan and liberal atmosphere of the pre-war years, while the return to traditional elements and a more representational style signify a more repressive and conservative political regime" (ibd.). He also underlines the ambivalence of the work of those artists who "often invoked the styles, themes, and tropes of the reactionary Right, but then subjected them to strategies such as parody, creolization, and métissage that fundamentally altered their valences and left them signifying otherwise" (Junyk 2013: 7). Consequently, Serge's works are an illustration of the emergence of resistance against radical authoritarian nationalism. Furthermore, Rhys seems to posit the modern metropolitan figure as the figure of the migrant. Helen Carr describes the atmosphere in pre-war times and concludes that "ranks are closing through fear; the marginals are ever more aggressively marginalized. Rhys's protagonists search for an escape from their isolation, from their unhomeliness: they look for love, for acceptance, for a chance to join" (Carr 1996: 63). She interprets Sasha's happiness when "Serge gives her hand a 'long hard shake' ('The touch of the human hand... I'd forgotten what it was like, the touch of the human hand') and says 'Amis'", as a moment where both individuals "shared the recognition of pain or loss" (ibd.). It becomes a necessity for those "casualties of the European world of 1937: people of the margins, of the ambiguous shadow land at society's edge" (ibd.) to fall back to narcissism as a means for self-preservation. This idea is reflected in Delmar's philosophy of life: "Why torment yourself? Why not take life just as it comes? You have the right to: you are not one of the guilty ones. [...] When you aren't rich or strong or powerful, you are not a guilty one" (Rhys 2000: 55). Sasha is half convinced by Delmar's philosophy, although she finds his suggestion of "disengagement, non-intervention" (Carr 1996: 61) tempting for it reminds herself of her own desire "to be left alone" (Rhys 2000: 37). In Sasha's case, her self-obsession is a means to distract her from the harshness that marginalized individuals undergo. Constantly reinventing herself through consumption of fashion commodities, Sasha attempts to "construct a new face, to make herself up, in both senses of the phrase" (Carr 1996: 58). Helen Carr sees Sasha and other Rhys' female protagonists as "creative artists" and their needs for self-creation as "their only steady occupation" (ibd.). Sasha's narcissistic absorption becomes meaningful and even beneficial in "keeping her sense of disintegration and worthlessness at bay" (ibd.). Carr points out that Sasha "organizes her life as a series of rituals; designed, like the rituals of long-term prisoners, to hold on to some control over her own being [...]; designed to evade hostility, fear, the destructive definitions of other people" (ibd.). Spending a good deal of the time looking at herself in the mirrors not only indicates Sasha's self-infatuation but according to the French psychoanalyst Jacques Lacan, Helen Carr explains "the image in the mirror is a misrecognition, yet even so essential in enabling the emergence of an 'I'" (Carr 1996: 59). Therefore, it can be concluded that it is through her narcissistic tendency that Sasha is able to resist losing sight of her 'self', and that she is able to escape the pressure and antagonism of pre-war Europe. The final scene of the novel constitutes an epiphany for Sasha, who becomes aware that she has misjudged René. Thinking at first that he intended to hurt her and steal her money, she tries to reverse the role and be the victimizer, hence she rejects "the gigolo's plea to go to bed with him [...] trying, in fact, to be hard and ruthless, to avenge her own earlier suffering at the hands of men on him" (Carr 1996: 66). However, when he leaves her without taking her money, she realizes that she has misjudged him, and that René is another of her alter egos. She is aware that she has unfairly denied him the compassion he longed for and that it was too late to make up for it. Consequently, when next, Sasha welcomes the 'ghost of the landing', the 'commis voyageur', an outcast she deeply despises from the start, she defies social expectations by showing a slant of generosity and offering "the touch of the human hand" to "another poor devil of a human" (Rhys 2000: 159); hence she reveals that she finally understands her neighbour's pain and loss. Her final utterance "Yes – yes – yes" is reminiscent of Molly Bloom's three yesses in James Joyce's *Ulysses*, when she finally accepts Leopold Bloom in her bed and thinking of their first meeting and the love she felt for him, she declares:

> I was a Flower of the mountain yes when I put the rose in my hair like the Andalusian girls used or shall I wear a red yes and how he kissed me under the Moorish Wall and I thought well as well him as another and then I asked him with my eyes to ask again yes and then he asked me would I yes to say yes my mountain flower and first I put my arms around him yes and drew him down to me so he could feel my breasts all perfume yes and his heart was going like mad and *yes* I said *yes* I will *Yes*. (*my emphasis*; Joyce 1998: 732)

This passage, which concludes Joyce's novel, has widely been read as an affirmation of life and rebirth. In *Good Morning, Midnight*, it becomes a narcissistic mother's demonstration of humanity, which arms her with the best weapon to resist the rise of nationalism and allows her to make up for her earlier rejection of René.

To conclude, Jean Rhys offers an unprecedented depiction of a narcissistic mother who tries to recover from her son's traumatic death and the series of humiliations she experienced through extreme consumption of fashion commodities. The author suggests a positive reading of the self-absorbed Sasha Jansen, when she illustrates her heroine's ability to show generosity and empathy for others. In fact, making a narcissistic mother the new face of the "prototypical figure of the flâneur" (Dell Amico 2005: 16), Rhys demonstrates through Sasha's enjoyment of luminal, alcohol, commodities and through her numerous visits in cafés, restaurants, theatres, and bars, a new kind of enjoyment for the crowd. Sasha is revealed to be an independent woman, who chooses to live her life as an Epicurean would. Her peripatetic stroll in the streets of Paris proves to be a means for moral growth, to artistically and critically investigate the society's meanders through her various encounters with social outcasts. Finally, Sasha as 'unwilling detective' serves Rhys' criticism of pre-war Europe and demonstrates how essential self-love is in order to resist the rise of nationalism.

7 From Modernism to Contemporary Literature: A Timeless Debate

CONCLUSION

Modernist literature is characterized by a departure from the previous optimism about progress that has pervaded the Victorian period. In their works, Modernist writers, such as D.H. Lawrence, James Joyce, Virginia Woolf and Jean Rhys, started criticizing middle-class Victorian values and attacking the long-established belief in national exceptionalism and in its mission to spread its model of civilization around the world, even though at times also showing nostalgia for the long-established convention. These writers express their loss of faith and their feeling of dissolution in their works, which were also tremendously influenced by the development in psychoanalysis as well as the important social and political reforms, such as the Married Women's Property Act of 1882, hence calling for an urgent reconsideration of women's position and role as spouse and mothers. All these important changes affecting the position of women in society are reflected through the portrayal of the female characters in the novels and short stories analysed in this book. Their controversial representation, especially of mother figures constitutes a means to attack Victorian values and tradition. Additionally, the outbreak of the Great War, which put an end to the triumphalism and optimism spread throughout the Victorian era, and the rapid disintegration of the British Empire, marked an important shift in the perception of the individual and his place in society. Indeed, these mother figures became the voice of the authors' acerbic criticism of the violence engendered by the war and the dangers of nationalistic pride. Accordingly, the evaluation of self-absorbed maternal figures in Modernist literature underlines this major shift in the intellectual current. While previous works on narcissistic mothers have essentially represented conflictual mother-child relationships as characterized primarily by maternal domination and child's submission, the present examination of self-centred maternal figures in Modernist literature allows a more positive interpretation of the mother-child dyad by considering the definitional nuances of the term 'narcissism'. Besides its oversimplified meaning of 'excessive admiration of oneself' and 'selfishness', it also initially refers to, as Sigmund Freud claimed, the essential part of an individual's 'normal' development, employed as a means for self-preservation by protecting a human being against illness. Therefore, breaking from previous ideas on motherhood, which persist in depicting narcissistic mothers' diabolical control over their children's subjectivity and stress their negative influence on the child's psychological development, these four major Modernist writers, D.H. Lawrence, James Joyce, Virginia Woolf and Jean Rhys, demonstrate that these mothers are able to care for their children. Even if mothers are often encouraged to construe their children as part of themselves, and are generally more attached to their children for they traditionally experience intensive physical intimacy (for instance, through giving birth and breast feeding) with the infant, and were and still are in most societies the primary nurturers, their narcissistic self can enable their children's personal development, and at the same time remains a means for self-preservation for these women. Thus, these four influential texts provide a more positive reading of narcissistic mother figures that has been previously conducted by considering the socio-political and socio-economic context of the time in shaping and encouraging these mothers' narcissistic behaviour. All four narratives illustrate the importance of being loved (including loving oneself) and loving others as a means for self-preservation.

D.H. Lawrence's novel *Sons and Lovers* (1913) depicts a mother who continuously seeks reparation for her injured self through her relationships with her sons, William and Paul. But if she has often been seen as a selfish and controlling mother, her wish for social ascension is far from being solely motivated by excessive greed but more by her protective maternal instinct. Aware of the dangers related to the mining job, she wishes, out of motherly love and concern, to spare her children from risking their life on a daily basis. As a woman of vision, she encourages her children's upward mobility as she is truly convinced that it can positively impact their life. Lastly, she proves to support and stimulate Paul's artistic path and as a result, at the end of the novel, the reader is left with a favourable depiction of the maternal figure. If in *Sons and Lovers*, the socio-economic parameter plays an essential role in establishing a more sympathetic image of the mother, in his short stories, James Joyce also seems to end up exonerating his narcissistic mothers by emphasizing the economic circumstances which contribute in triggering and sustaining mothers' narcissistic injury, hence pushing them to seek reparative measures as a means for self-preservation. Yet, in "A Painful Case", by also providing an example of damaging narcissism through the character of James Duffy, Joyce offers a direct comparison to the benevolent narcissistic mother embodied through the character of Emily Sinico. Duffy's selfishness contributes in morally elevating the mother figure. At the same time, it distinguishes, in a manner analogous to Freud, between the 'healthy' and 'unhealthy' type of narcissism. This representation of different forms of narcissism is also expressed through the novels of Virginia Woolf and Jean Rhys. Through the fictional Mrs. Ramsay in *To the Lighthouse*, Virginia Woolf confirms that self-absorbed mothers are still capable of loving and nurturing their children and that one does not necessarily exclude the other. Woolf shows that in the case of Mrs. Ramsay, narcissism allows the character to protect herself from the overwhelming demands and constraints that the Victorian principles enforce onto women, especially on mothers who are expected to be self-sacrificing and selfless at all times. Woolf reveals the struggle women undergo in their effort to break from the past in order to embrace a new future and offers an alternative solution when she points out that women need to negotiate their place within the system rather than completely parting from it. Also, the novel examines the negative type of narcissism in relation to the violence occasioned by the Great War, by stressing human beings' objectification and dehumanization. This question is also explored in Jean Rhys' novel through Sasha Jansen's stroll in the city. Sasha embodies a mother who tries to recover from the traumatic death of her infant and multiple humiliations she experienced through excessive consumption of alcohol, drugs, sex and fashion commodities. Against all expectation, she shows empathy and concerns for others. Rhys redefines the figure of the 'flâneur', who becomes the embodiment of the new independent woman according to the Rhysian standard. Through her walk in the city of Paris, the 'flâneur' investigates the society of the time and mirrors Rhys' criticism of pre-war Europe by underlining the essential role of self-love in the resistance against the rise of nationalism.

If today, repressive narratives about mothers' obligations towards their infant continue to advocate the image of the ideal mother as being selfless and compassionate, and still dominate the literary and artistic scene, examples of mothers who do not match this utopian definition are more and more frequently seen. This tendency reflects an important social shift in the sexual division of labour, triggered by recent economic and political development, specific to a particular period and society. The study of the mother-child relationship still presently and continuously preoccupies psychoanalysis, sociology, gender studies and literature, which attempt to identify the way society and culture affect the mother's experience of child rearing. If in this book, the focus is primarily on the representation of mothers in Western Modernist literature, the on-going contemporary debate around the concept of 'Tiger Mother' in Chinese culture or 'Kyōiku Mama' in modern Japanese society could potentially be considered as a significant add-on to the present discussion on narcissistic mothers. The terms 'Tiger Mother' and 'Kyōiku Mama' refer to a harsh and demanding mother who pushes her children to be successful both academically and professionally, for they relate the idea of accomplishment to education and intellectual achievements. The term 'Tiger Mother' recently became the centre of attention following Amy Chua's memoir *Battle Hymn of the Tiger Mother* (2011), in which she describes the harsh parental practices she imposes on her daughters in order to push them towards academic excellence. Her pedagogical methods have aroused mixed feelings among the public. While some have regarded these mothers' pedagogical practices as psychologically abusive, and have blamed them for their children's physical and mental health problems, such as "stammering, poor appetite, [and] school phobia" (Ochiai 1997: 51), others have attempted to understand the motive behind such an education. They actually concluded that these mothers' high expectations stem from parental affection and concern for their children, along with their strong desire to actively participate and anticipate their children's success. However, they tend to perceive their children's future through the lens of their own experiences, and their own aspirations. In the same way as the mothers in *Dubliners* and *Sons and Lovers* advocate social ascension, 'Tiger Mothers' and 'Kyōiku Mama' acknowledge the role of education in enabling promising career prospects, which in turn, they are convinced, play an important role in social mobility. The pejorative and stereotypical term 'Kyōiku Mama' or 'Education Mama', which evokes the idea of an intensely competitive and demanding mother figure, is also nuanced by a portrayal of these mothers as self-sacrificing, both career and personal aspirations, in order to devote themselves to their children's education. A recent article written by Tony Dickensheets examines the role of 'Education Mama' and tends to offer a more favourable picture of these mothers by emphasizing the role they played in turning Japan into the 'economic giant' it became during the post-war era, through relentless dedication in pushing their children towards academic success and instilling in them the work ethic of the stereotypical salaryman. Dickensheets writes that "behind every great man – or salaryman – is a great woman" (Dickensheets 1996: para.1). Finally, it seems that these women's role in the nation's education, and thereby, their country's post-war recovery, needs to be acknowledged. Thus, when taking into account the issue of narcissistic mothers, it is essential to consider the social, political as well as economic context of the time (also culturally specific), which contributes in offering a more nuanced image of these women. While those mothers are regarded as social phenomenon and have been the object of controversial debate over the years because they still endorse more responsibility in the children's upbringing and are often held accountable for their children's academic and social achievements, to this day little work has been conducted on the issue of narcissistic fathers, which could provide another angle to explore the arguments on child's development.

Works Cited

Angier, Carole (1992): *Jean Rhys*. England: Penguin Books.
Auden, W. H. (1976): "In Memory of Sigmund Freud". *Collected Poems*. Ed. Edward Mendelson. London: Faber & Faber.
Bazin, Nancy T. & Jane Hamovit Lauter (1992): "Woolf's Keen Sensitivity to War". *Virginia Woolf and War: Fiction, Reality, and Myth*. Ed. Mark Hussey. Syracuse: Syracuse University Press, p. 14-39.
Beards, Richard D. (1974): *"Sons and Lovers* as Bildungsroman". *College Literature*. 1:3, p. 204-217.
Beck, Warren (1969): *Joyce's 'Dubliners': Substance, Vision, and Art*. Durham, N.C.: Duke University Press.
Becket, Fiona (2002): *The Complete Critical Guide to D.H. Lawrence*. New York: Routledge.
Bell, Ilona (1986): "Haunted by Great Ghosts: Virginia Woolf and *To the Lighthouse*". *Biography*. 9:2, p. 150-175.
Bell, Michael (2001): "Lawrence and Modernism". *The Cambridge Companion to D.H. Lawrence*. Ed. Anne Fernihough. Cambridge: Cambridge University Press, p. 179-196.
Bell, Quentin (1973): *Virginia Woolf: A Biography*. London: The Hogarth Press.
Benjamin, Walter (1985): *Charles Baudelaire: A Lyric Poet in the Era of High Capitalism*. London: Verso.
Benjamin, Walter (2006): *The Writer of Modern Life: Essays on Charles Baudelaire*. United States: Harvard University Press.

Berman, Jeffrey (1990): *Narcissism and the Novel.* New York & London: New York University Press.
Black, Michael (2005): "Form: Narrative Structure". *D.H. Lawrence's 'Sons and Lovers': A Casebook.* Ed. John Worthen & Andrew Harrison. Oxford: Oxford University Press.
Bloom, Barbara (1990): *The Reign of Narcissism.* Stuttgart: Württembergischer Kunstverein Stuttgart.
Bloom, Harold (1988): *James Joyce's 'Dubliners'.* New York: Chelsea House Publishers.
Blotner, Joseph (1970): "Mythic Patterns in *To the Lighthouse*" (1956). *Virginia Woolf, "To the Lighthouse": A Collection of Critical Essays.* Ed. Morris Beja. London: Macmillan, p. 169-188.
Boulding, Kaitlyn (2013): "Plato's Eros Reflected in Ovid's Narcissus". *Pseudo Dionysius Journal.* Vol.15, p. 1-12.
Boulton, James T. (2002): *The Letters of D.H. Lawrence.* By D.H. Lawrence. Cambridge: Cambridge University Press. Vol.1.
Bowlby, Rachel (1985): *Just Looking: Consumer Culture in Dreiser, Gissing and Zola.* New York: Methuen.
Bradbury, Nicola (1994): "Introduction". *To the Lighthouse.* By Virginia Woolf. London: Wordsworth Classics, p. v-xvi.
Briggs, Julia (2011): "Virginia Woolf Meets Sigmund Freud". *CANVAS.* Issue 18.
Brown, Terence (1992): "Introduction". *Dubliners.* By James Joyce. England: Penguin Books, p. vii-xlviii.
Carr, Helen (1996): *Jean Rhys.* Plymouth, United Kingdom: Northcote House.
Chambers, Ross (1999): *Loiterature.* Lincoln & London: University of Nebraska Press.
Chodorow, Nancy (1978): *The Reproduction of Mothering: Psychoanalysis and the Sociology of Gender.* California: University of California Press.
Chua, Amy (2011): *Battle Hymn of the Tiger Mother.* Great Britain: Bloomsbury Publishing.

Cixous, Hélène (1972): *The Exile of James Joyce*. Trans. Sally A. J. Purcell. New York: David Lewis.

Conlon, John J. (1982): *Walter Pater and the French Tradition*. London & Toronto: Bucknell University Press.

Daiches, David (1970): "The Semi-Transparent Envelope". *Twentieth Century Interpretations of 'To the Lighthouse': Selection of Critical Essays*. Ed. Thomas A. Vogler. New Jersey: Englewood Cliffs, Prentice Hall, p. 58-69.

Daleski, Hillel M. (1988): "The Son and the Artist". *D.H. Lawrence's 'Sons and Lovers'*. Ed. Harold Bloom. New York: Chelsea House Publishers, p. 23-45.

Daly, Macdonald (2005): "Relationship and Class in *Sons and Lovers*". *D.H. Lawrence's 'Sons and Lovers': A Casebook*. Ed. John Worthen & Andrew Harrison. Oxford: Oxford University Press.

Dell' Amico, Carol (2005): *Colonialism and the Modernist Moment in the Early Novels of Jean Rhys*. New York & London: Routledge.

DeVault, Christopher M. (2010): "Love and Socialism in Joyce's "A Painful Case": A Buberian Reading." *College Literature*. 37: 2, p. 78-102.

Dever, Carolyn (1998): "Virginia Woolf's "Victorian Novel"". *Death and the Mother from Dickens to Freud: Victorian Fiction and the Anxiety of Origins*. Cambridge: Cambridge University Press, p. 203-212.

Dickensheets, Tony (1996): "The Role of the Education Mama". *Japan Quarterly*, p. 73.

Ellis, Havelock (1942): *Studies in the Psychology of Sex*. New York: Random House.

Ellmann, Richard (1982): *James Joyce*. New York: Oxford University Press.

Ellmann, Richard (1975): *Selected Letters of James Joyce*. By James Joyce. London: Faber.

Emery, Mary Lou (1982): *Modernism and the Marginal Women: a Sociocritical Approach to the Novels of Jean Rhys*. Stanford University Press: California.

Farr, Judith (1990): "D.H. Lawrence's Mother as Sleeping Beauty: The "Still Queen" of his Poems and Fictions". *Modern Fiction Studies*. 36:2, p. 195-209.

Fest, Kerstin (2009): *And All Women Mere Players? Performance and Identity in Dorothy Richardson, Jean Rhys and Radclyffe Hall.* Braumüller: Vienna, Austria.

Finney, Brian (1990): *D.H. Lawrence: 'Sons and Lovers'.* London: Penguin Books.

Fliess, Robert (1970): *Ego and Body Ego: Contributions to their Psychoanalytic Psychology.* New York: International Universities Press.

Forrester, Viviane (2015): *Virginia Woolf: A Portrait.* Translated by Jody Gladding. New York: Columbia University Press.

Freud, Sigmund (2010): *Beyond the Pleasure Principle.* USA: Pacific Publishing Studio.

Freud, Sigmund (1916): "Lecture XXIII: The Paths to the Formation of Symptoms". *Standard Edition*, Vol. XVI. London: The Hogarth Press.

Freud, Sigmund (2013): *On Narcissism: An Introduction.* Great Britain: Read Books Ltd.

Froula, Christina (2005): *Virginia Woolf and the Bloomsbury Avant-Garde: War, Civilization, Modernity.* New York: Columbia University Press.

Gillies, Mary Ann & Aurelea Mahood (2007): *Modernist Literature: An Introduction.* Edinburgh, Great Britain: Edinburgh University Press.

Goldman, Jane (2006): *The Cambridge Introduction to Virginia Woolf.* United Kingdom: Cambridge University Press.

Gordon, Lyndall (1984): *Virginia Woolf: A Writer's Life.* Oxford: Oxford University Press.

Gorman, Herbert (1941): *James Joyce: A Definitive Biography.* New York: Rhinehart & Company.

Graham-Dixon, Andrew (2003): "Rude Awakening". *The Telegraph.*

http://www.telegraph.co.uk/culture/art/3605916/Rude-awakening. html. Accessed 13 June 2016.

Henke, Suzette A. (1980): "Feminist Perspectives on James Joyce". *The Canadian Journal of Irish Studies*. 6:1, p. 14-22.

Herbert, James D. (1995): "The View of the Trocadéro: The Real Subject of the Exposition Internationale, Paris, 1937". *Assemblage*. 26, p. 94-112.

Hopkin, William E. (1957): *D.H. Lawrence: A Composite Biography*. Ed. By Edward Nehls. Madison: The University of Wisconsin Press, p. 21-25.

Hussey, Mark (1992): *Virginia Woolf and War, Fiction, Reality, and Myth*. Syracuse: Syracuse University Press.

Jackson, John W. & Bernard McGinley (1993): *James Joyce's 'Dubliners'*. By James Joyce. New York: St. Martin's Press.

Jensen, Katharine A. (2011): *Uneasy Possessions: Mother-Daughter Dilemma in French Women's Writings, 1671-1928*. Newark: University of Delaware Press.

Johnson, Jeri (2000): "Introduction". *Dubliners*. By James Joyce. Oxford: Oxford World's Classics.

Jones, Ernest (1949): "Hamlet and Oedipus". New York Norton Publisher.

Joyce, James (2000): *Dubliners*. Ed. Jeri Johnson. Oxford: Oxford World's Classics.

Joyce, James (2001): *A Portrait of the Artist as a Young Man*. Kent, Great Britain: Wordsworth Classics.

Joyce, James (1969): *Stephen Hero: Part of the First Draft of 'A Portrait of the Artist as a Young Man'*. Ed. Theodore Spencer, John J. Slocum & Herbert Cahoon. Bedford Square, London: Jonathan Cape.

Joyce, James (1998): *Ulysses*. Ed. Jeri Johnson. Oxford: Oxford World's Classics.

Junyk, Ihor (2013): *Foreign Modernism: Cosmopolitanism, Identity, and Style in Paris*. Toronto: University of Toronto Press.

Karl, Alissa G. (2009): *Modernism and the Marketplace: Literary Culture and Consumer Capitalism in Rhys, Woolf, Stein, and Nella Larsen.* New York: Routledge.

Kolstø, Pål (2007): "The 'Narcissism of Minor Differences' – Theory: Can it Explain Ethnic Conflict?". *Filozofija i Društvo.* 18:2, p. 153-171.

Kristeva, Julia (1989): *Black Sun: Depression and Melancholia.* New York: Columbia University Press.

Kuttner, Alfred B. (1916): "*Sons and Lovers*: A Freudian Appreciation". *Psychoanalytic Review 3,* p. 295-317.

Lawrence, David H. (1994): *The Complete Poems of D.H. Lawrence.* Hertfordshire: Wordsworth Editions.

Lawrence, David H. (1930): *Fantasia of the Unconscious.* London: Martin Secker Ltd.

Lawrence, David H. (1982): *The Letters of D.H. Lawrence.* Ed. Georges J. Zytaruk & James T. Boulton. Cambridge: Cambridge University Press. Vol. 2.

Lawrence, David H. (1989): *The Letters of D.H. Lawrence.* Ed. James T. Boulton & Lindeth Vasey. Cambridge: Cambridge University Press. Vol. 5.

Lawrence, David H. (2004): *Psychoanalysis and the Unconscious* and *Fantasia of the Unconscious.* Ed. by Bruce Steele. Cambridge; New York: Cambridge University Press.

Lawrence, David H. (1989): *The Rainbow.* Ed. Mark Kinkead-Weekes. Cambridge & New York: Cambridge University Press.

Lawrence, David H. (1988): *Reflections on the Death of a Porcupine and Other Essays.* Ed. Michael Herbert & James T. Boulton. Cambridge: Cambridge University Press.

Lawrence, David H. (1992): *Sons and Lovers.* Ed. Helen Baron & Carl Baron. New York, USA & Victoria, Australia: Cambridge University Press.

Lawrence, David H. (1987): *Women in Love.* Ed. David Farmer, Lindeth Vasey & John Worthen. Cambridge: Cambridge University Press.

Lawrence, Karen (1990): "Joyce and Feminism". *The Cambridge Companion to James Joyce*. Cambridge: Cambridge University Press, p. 237-258.
Lee, Hermione (2010). *Body Parts: Essays on Life-Writing*. New York: Random House.
Lee, Hermione (1996): *Virginia Woolf*. Great Britain: Chatto & Windus.
Menninger, Karl A. (1942): *Love against Hate*. New York: Harcourt, Brace & Company.
Miller, Alice (1986): "Depression and Grandiosity as Related Forms of Narcissistic Disturbances". *Essential Papers on Narcissism*. Ed. Andrew P. Morrison. New York: New York University Press, p. 323-347.
Moore, Harry T. (1951): *The Life and Work of D.H. Lawrence*. New York: Twayne.
Morrison, Andrew P. (1986): *Essential Papers on Narcissism*. New York: New York University Press.
Nalbantian, Suzanne (1994): "The Stylised Quotidian in James Joyce". *Aesthetic Autobiography: From Life to Art in Marcel Proust, James Joyce, Virginia Woolf and Anaïs Nin*. Great Britain: Macmillan Press, p. 100-133.
Nehls, Edward (1957): *D.H. Lawrence: A Composite Biography*. Madison: The University of Wisconsin Press.
Nietzsche, Friedrich (2017): *Morgenröthe*. Nikosia, Cyprus: TP Verone Publishing House.
Norris, Margot (1997): "Narrative Bread Pudding: Joyce's "The Boarding House"". *New Perspectives on 'Dubliners'*. Ed. Mary Power. Amsterdam-Atlanta, GA: Rodopi, p. 143-166.
Norris, Margot (2003): *Suspicious Readings of Joyce's 'Dubliners'*. Philadelphia: University of Pennsylvania Press.
Ochiai, Emiko (1997): *The Japanese Family System in Transition: A Sociological Analysis of Family Change in Postwar Japan*. Tokyo: LTCB International Library Foundation.

Oheix, Kevin (2013): *Yeats, Joyce and Mother Ireland.* Norderstedt, Germany: Grin Press.
Paige, Linda Rohrer (1995): "James Colored Portraits Joyce's Darkly of 'Mother' in *Dubliners.*" *Studies in Short Fiction.* 3:2, p. 329-340.
Panken, Shirley (1987): *Virginia Woolf and the Lust of Creation.* Albany, New York: State University of New York Press.
Pease, Allison (2015): *The Cambridge Companion to: 'To the Lighthouse'.* New York: Cambridge University Press.
Pedersen, Glenn (1958): "Vision in *To the Lighthouse*". *Modern Language Association.* 73:5, p. 585-600.
Peiss, Kathy (1998): *Hope in a Jar: The Making of America's Beauty Culture.* New York: Henry Holt.
Pizzichini, Lilian (2009): *The Blue Hour: A Portrait of Jean Rhys.* London: Bloomsbury Publishing.
Plato (1989): *Symposium.* Indianapolis, Indiana: Hackett Publishing.
Poole, Roger (1992): "'We all put up with you Virginia': Irreceivable Wisdom about War". *Virginia Woolf and War: Fiction, Reality, and Myth.* Ed. Mark Hussey. Syracuse: Syracuse University Press, p. 79-100.
Power, Mary (1997): *New Perspectives on 'Dubliners'.* Amsterdam-Atlanta, GA: Rodopi.
Proudfit, Sharon W. (1971): "Lily Briscoe's Painting: A Key to Personal Relationships in *To the Lighthouse*". Wayne State University Press. 13:1, p. 26-38.
Raitt, Suzanne (1990): *Virginia Woolf's 'To the Lighthouse'.* Hertfordshire: Harvester Wheatsheaf.
Rhys, Jean (1985): "After Leaving Mr Mackenzie". *Jean Rhys: The Complete Novels.* New York & London: W.W Norton, p. 235-344.
Rhys, Jean (2000): *Good Morning, Midnight.* London, England: Penguin Classics.
Rhys, Jean (2016): *Smile Please: An Unfinished Autobiography.* United Kingdom: Penguin Modern Classics.
Rhys, Jean (1982): *Wide Sargasso Sea.* New York: Norton.

Ruderman, Judith (1984): *D.H. Lawrence and the Devouring Mother*. Durham, N.C: Duke University Press.
Rylance, Rick (2001): "Ideas, Histories, Generations and Beliefs". *The Cambridge Companion to D.H. Lawrence*. Ed. Anne Fernihough. Cambridge: Cambridge University Press, p. 15-31.
Sagar, Keith (1989): "Introduction". *Sons and Lovers*. England: Penguin Books, p. 11-28.
Sagar, Keith (2003): *D.H. Lawrence's Paintings*. By D.H. Lawrence. London: Chaucer Press.
Salgădo, Gămini (1996): *D.H. Lawrence: 'Sons and Lovers'*. London: Edward Arnold Publishers Ltd.
Savory, Elaine (2009): *The Cambridge Introduction to Jean Rhys*. New York: The Cambridge University Press.
Schapiro, Barbara (1999): "The Dread and repulsiveness of the Wild: D.H. Lawrence and Shame". *Scenes of Shame: Psychoanalysis, Shame, and Writing*. Ed. Joseph Adamson & Hilary Clark. Albany: State University of New York Press.
Silver, Brenda R. (2009): "Mothers, Daughters, Mrs. Ramsay: Reflections". *Women's Studies Quarterly*. 37: ¾, p. 259-274.
Sklenicka, Carol (1991): *D.H. Lawrence and the Child*. Columbia and London: University of Missouri Press.
Sotirova, Violeta (2011): *D.H. Lawrence and Narrative Viewpoint*. Ed. Daniel McIntyre. UK: University of Huddersfield.
Spencer, Roy (1980): *D.H. Lawrence Country: A Portrait of his Early Life and Background with Illustrations, Maps and Guides*. London: Cecil Woolf Publishers.
Stanback, Emily B. (2013): "Peripatetic in the City: De Quincey's *Confessions of an English Opium-Eater* and the Birth of the Flâneur". *Literature Compass*. 10:2, p. 146-161.
Stewart, Jack (2005): "Forms and Expressions in *Sons and Lovers*". *D.H. Lawrence's 'Sons and Lovers': A Casebook*. Ed. John Worthen & Andrew Harrison. New York: Oxford University Press, p. 155-188.

Strouse, L.W. (1981): "Virginia Woolf and Her 'Voyage Out.'" *American Imago*, 38, p. 185-202.

Taussig, Michael (1993): "Maleficium: State Fetishism". *Fetishism as Cultural Discourse*. Ed. Emily Apter and William Pietz. Ithica: Cornell University Press, p. 217-234.

Tedlock, Ernest W. (1965): *D.H. Lawrence and 'Sons and Lovers': Sources and Criticism*. New York: New York University Press.

Vadillo, Ana Parejo (2015): "Generational Difference in *To the Lighthouse*". *The Cambridge Companion to: 'To the Lighthouse'*. Ed. Allison Pease. New York: Cambridge University Press, p. 122-135.

Van Ghent, Dorothy (1988): "On *Sons and Lovers*". *D.H. Lawrence's 'Sons and Lovers'*. Ed. Harold Bloom. New York: Chelsea House Publishers, p. 5-22.

Van Rhee, Kirsten Vera (2011): *James Joyce: The Situation of Women in 'Dubliners' in Special View of "Eveline"*. Norderstedt, Germany: GRIN Press.

Winston, Janet (2009): *Woolf's 'To the Lighthouse': A Reader's Guide*. London: Continuum International Publishing Group.

Woolf, Virginia (1949): *A Room of One's Own*. London: The Hogarth Press.

Woolf, Virginia (1976): *Moments of Being*. London: The University Press Sussex.

Woolf, Virginia (1992): *Mrs Dalloway*. London: Penguin Classics.

Woolf, Virginia (1975): *The Letters of Virginia Woolf*. Ed. Nigel Nicolson & Joanne Trautmann. New York & London: Harcourt Brace Jovanovich Publisher.

Woolf, Virginia (2006): *To the Lighthouse*. Ed. David Bradshaw. New York: Oxford University Press.

Worthen, John (1992): *D.H. Lawrence: The Early Years 1885-1912*. Great Britain: Cambridge University Press.

Yildiz, Firat (2013): "Women Types in *To the Lighthouse* and *Mrs. Dalloway*". *Sosyal Bilimler Dergisi*. XV:2, p. 18-24.

Zimring, Rishona (2000): "The Make-up of Jean Rhys's Fiction". *NOVEL: A Forum of Fiction*. 33:2, p. 212-234.